Be Inspired

Be Inspiring

Blessings + Butterflies

Vanessa

☺ x x

I trust you will enjoy the messages and thoughts in my book. As it is the first edition we have found there are some spelling mistakes and 29th January is missing from the print. Knowing you will still benefit from the energy in these words, I thank you for your understanding.

29th January

If you bring love. Whatever your fate is, whatever the heck happens, you say "This is what I need". It may look like a wreck, but go at it as though it were an opportunity, a challenge. If you bring love to that moment – not discouragement – you will find the strength is there. Any disaster that you can survive is an improvement in your character, your stature and your life. What a privilege! This is when the spontaneity of your own nature will have a chance to flow. Then, when looking back at your life, you will see that the moments which seemed to be great failures followed by wreckage were the incidents that shaped the life you have now. You'll see that this is really true. Nothing can happen to you that is not positive. Even though it looks and feels at the moment like a negative crisis, it is not!

Butterfly Whispers

One Moment, One Thought
Can Change Your Day

Vanessa Stottor

BALBOA PRESS

A DIVISION OF HAY HOUSE

Balboa Press books may be ordered through booksellers or by contacting:

Balboa Press
A Division of Hay House
1663 Liberty Drive
Bloomington, IN 47403
www.balboapress.com
1 (877) 407-4847

Printed in the United States of America.

ISBN: 978-1-4525-8472-0 (sc)
ISBN: 978-1-4525-8473-7 (e)

Library of Congress Control Number: 2013918621

Balboa Press rev. date: 11/25/2013

My heartfelt thanks go to all who made this book possible:

Tania Cooper—If it wasn't for your phone call, it may have not begun! Thank you.

Marilyn Messik—It was your idea to turn my phone line into a book. Thank you for your vision.

June Dean, Lynn Stainthorpe and Kelly Baines—for many a session around the table and on the phone encouraging me to carry on. Thank you

Cathy Gallagher – Your endless patience in typing up every single word from my scribbled notes – I couldn't have done it without you! You are a star!

Vanessa Emery—Your continued support and brilliant artwork. You design what I visualise and you are spot on. Thank you.

Lyn Halvorsen—A lifelong friend with a talent for simple yet perfect illustrations. You are heaven sent. Thank you.

Donna Ashcroft—for you truly write what I think and say it better in such profound words. Thank you for helping me with your gift.

Jacqueline Rogers—My confidant and Visionary buddy, Thank you for holding my hand and guiding me from rose bud to full bloom.

Balboa Press—Every single one of you have been incredibly accommodating. Your enthusiasm and encouragement is second to none. Thank you.

Abbie, my sister and best friend—I love you for always supporting everything I do and for loving me as you do.

Mum and Dad—words are never enough to express how grateful I am for your unconditional love, support and for all of life's lessons you have taught me along the way. This book is all because of you. Thank you from the bottom of my heart.

Liberty, my angel, and Jodi, my prince—God truly blessed me with you two wonderful children. You are the reason I do what I do. Thank you for your input with some of the messages in this book. You are two remarkable people that brighten every day.

Brian, my husband, my soul mate and my inspiration—You are my rock. I thank God for the blessing of you daily. Thank you for waking me up from my keyboard, your gentle whispers of 'I love you' and more importantly for believing in me. I dedicate this book to you. I love you too.

1 January

Love is the only way forward. Today is the beginning of a new year.

As we glance back in our rear-view mirror and notice our year gone before, there were times we cherished and times that were challenging. When we look closely, I'm sure love played a part in all our memories, good or bad, and from all types of people. Look more closely, and you'll notice love is the only way forward. Love is the easiest thing to carry around. And the more you give away, the more you gain. You cannot help but feel happy when you feel love. As we travel through the year ahead, may we do so with love and be remembered as a loving person. Love is the main ingredient of life, and when we realise that, it will change everything. Start by loving *you!*

2 January

It's a Wonderful Life: the title of one of the best films ever made. The story of a man who has lost his way in life, and in his darkest hour asks for guidance. A guardian angel shows up and reminds him what a wonderful life he does actually have. He shows him what a difference he has made to others and that his life has been and is of great importance.

When you see your world without you in it, it definitely makes you appreciate what you have. The man was reminded of what a wonderful life he had and that a man is no failure when he has friends.

Enjoy your wonderful life!

3 January

The shape of life! Life is a cycle . . . a journey. Along the ride we have findings. Things we learn about ourselves and others help guide us on our journey through life.

By journeying through our daily lives, we move on. We must keep moving to progress. Whenever we take a knock, it's important we keep moving. However, there are certain parts of times in our journey where we need to wait! Spend time contemplating our journey so far and the road yet to travel. To be patient and wait are important parts of our journey. Collect our findings and plan where to travel next. For us to truly grow, we need to step out. Be brave and courageous. It's all part of the cycle.

The shape of life is a cycle . . . a journey!

4 January

When all is going well, it's great. But how do we cope when we get knocked off-track? This is often the tell-tale sign of how our lives move forward. Are we the kind of people who jump up and down, screaming, "It's not fair," and blame others around us, or do we have a 'funny five minutes' over it and work out how to get ourselves back on track? Interestingly enough, I was told of a way to cope, confront, and deal with a problem or issue earlier today only to come home and have to put it into practice. Write down your worries or the problem; write down how you think you could solve it or make it right. Write down who or what may help you get there. The more you write down, the more space you clear in your head, making room for a solution. Makes perfect sense, and it really helped. Something that's definitely worth a try. Here's hoping you have a problem-free day.

5 January

Have you ever had your heart set on something you really wanted? Whether it be a holiday, a dream house, a special person, a certain piece of jewellery, or a handbag, there are always special things we would like to have but sometimes seem out of reach. The law of attraction tells us if we visualise what it is we want, it will materialise. Simply cut out a picture of what you would like to have, and put it where you will see it every day. By reminding ourselves daily of what we would like to have, the mind gets busy in trying to make this happen. *Feel* what it will be like to have it, and truly believe it will be yours. Daily visualise to materialise.

6 January

If we have anything bothering us, we tend to talk to friends about it. If we talk to too many people, we can sometimes get too many conflicting bits of advice and then feel worse off and confused. Talk to fewer people, and only talk to people you love and who love you. This will make things a lot clearer in your head. You will get more suitable advice, as these people know you better and care about helping you solve the situation. You will then have more confidence in your actions, knowing your loved ones helped you reach a decision. When something is bothering you, ask only the people you love and who love you to help you sort it through.

7 January

A traveller once asked a wise man sitting at a city's walls what the people there were like. "What are the people like in the city you came from?" asked the wise man.

The stranger pondered a moment. "They're generous and kind, they're patient and good folk," he replied.

"Well, that's how you'll find them here," the wise man said. A few days later, another traveller came to the city and asked the wise man the same question. "What are the people like in the city you come from?" the wise man wanted to know.

Again there was some hesitation. "The people are fairly mean," he said. "They're a grumpy lot and pretty miserable."

"Well," said the wise man, "that's just how you'll find people here."

In other words, people respond to how you behave. Laugh, and the world laughs with you!

8 January

It's the eye of the tiger, it's the thrill of the fight
Risin' up to the challenge of our rivals
It's the last-known survivor that stalks his prey in the night
And he's watching us all with the eye of the tiger!

Jim Peterik and Frankie Sullivan

How hungry are you? Not for your next meal but for what you want in your life.

The thrill of actually getting out there and fighting for what you want; rising up to the challenge of our rivals. It is healthy to be competitive, but remember to run your own race. The one who goes the extra mile wins.

It's all about whether or not we are willing to fight for what we want, willing to step up to the plate, and willing to be the best we can possibly be.

9 January

You are you because of your God-given talents and your natural abilities. Your talents will carry you through life and can set you apart from the next person. Use your talents to help others and to make their world and your world a better place. Your talents make you unique. Collectively, they can be very powerful, motivating, and inspiring. Your talents have gotten you this far, so rely on them to take you further. They are what is natural about you.

You are who you are because of your talents.

10 January

Celebrate even the smallest successes. They are all steps in the right direction. A journey of a thousand miles consists of small steps. Each step is a success. If you have a goal to earn an extra £1,000 and in the next month you earn £400, celebrate it! Turn on the music and dance round the room, go out to dinner, or simply congratulate yourself in the mirror. When you reach your goal, have a bigger celebration. Celebrate in a way that is nurturing to you. Congratulate yourself. We tend to forget to celebrate or feel good about our progress and then our goals become too far in the distance.

Life is a celebration! Enjoy the celebration!

11 January

The owner of a shop was asked, "How's business?"

She answered, "It's doing OK. Just about pays the bills." One day when she heard what she was saying, she wondered if business was slow because of what she thought. So from then on, when someone asked her how business was, she said, "Fantastic! It earns me a fortune." She then had a thriving business that earns her a fortune.

Simply adjusting our words can make all the difference. Positive words, such as 'love,' 'success,' and 'pride' have higher energy levels. Negative words, such as 'anger,' 'fight,' and 'hurt' have lower energy levels. Our choice of words can affect our very being. Make an effort today to only use positive words; it's not as easy as it looks. Instead of, "Why are we always late in the morning?", say, "It's great being early in the morning." Change your words to change your world.

12 January

Some people are just unhappy, but they are not unhappy enough to do anything about it! We all know people who go from day to day, week to week, year to year plodding on but not really that happy. They don't really know they are unhappy. We do, as we hear them talk about their lives, families, friends, and jobs. Their existence has become such a habit, they don't realise there may be another option out there. But they are not unhappy enough to do anything about it. What will be their trigger?

Have you ever been so unhappy or fed up that something snapped inside you and made you realise things had to change? Everyone has a trigger point. Sometimes we need to pull it ourselves and not wait for someone else to do so. Be happy today and all days!

13 January

"Don't put off to tomorrow what can be done today." I think we may all be guilty of this one. "I'll do it tomorrow." I just say to myself "DIN-DIN"—Do it now-do it now! Procrastination is such an easy state to fall into and the hardest to get out of. Bite the bullet, as they say, and do it now! When we do, we feel so much better and accomplish so much more. We have all started our year with great intentions, lots of list making, new routines, and so on, but it's about now when we can feel ourselves slipping back into our old ways. Don't! Create a new habit. Do it now! On your list, do the hardest things first, and the simpler things take care of themselves. Practice it for a few days and you'll see. Be part of the DIN-DIN Club, and do it now! "Don't put off to tomorrow what can be done today."

14 January

Choose to be happy now! Regardless of how much money you earn, where you live, or achievements you have accomplished, if you are looking for happiness outside yourself, you'll never find it. I'm sure we're all guilty of saying, "I'll be happy when . . . I'll be happy if . . ."

Come back to the truth, and the truth is that true joy is in the here and now, in this moment. It all begins with you. No one can give it to you or take it away. Don't ever forget that happiness is an inside job. Practice being naturally happy and secure within yourself, and you'll notice success flowing to you. Success and wealth flow to those who don't need it to be happy. Choose to be happy now!

15 January

Did you ever know that you're my hero,
and everything I'd like to be?
I can fly higher than an eagle,
'cause you are the wind beneath my wings.

Jeff Silbar and Larry Henley

Do we ever stop to think of our successes as successes because there was someone who was the wind beneath our wings? Someone who helped us fly higher than an eagle? We must never take for granted the help we receive, however big or small, for all our achievements. Some people don't choose to enjoy their moment of glory in public; to some people, being the wind beneath your wings is enough.

Be grateful for every gust of wind that helps you along your way, because even a handheld kite would be a flop without a gust of wind to carry it to great heights. "I can fly higher than an eagle, 'cause you are the wind beneath my wings."

16 January

It's another world! While I was at work, I was involved in a conversation about boats with three women and one of their husbands. The couple in the conversation was looking to buy a new boat. We were shown pictures of some amazing boats, and the one they liked was around half a million pounds. The husband told us a story about a new boat owner he knew, and they had all been invited out for the weekend on this boat. So off they went. The captain of the boat, his friend, needed fuel before the main part of their journey. After "filling her up," he was given a bill of £125,000. I gasped, obviously a novice about boats. These boats were worth millions of pounds; they were beautiful and exquisite boats. It's another world! I did come away with a smile, because these people were as passionate about their boats as I am about what I am able to provide for my family. It's *your* world you need to be passionate about!

17 January

A new chapter! The other day I drove past a family moving into their new home. I thought, *How exciting: starting a new chapter in their lives.* The beginning of a new year is a perfect time to begin a new chapter. But why wait 'til the beginning of the year? why wait 'til Monday? Why wait until we think the time is right? Start a new chapter every day. We all love things when they are new; they excite us! They give us the drive and momentum to carry on.

Starting over or starting anew means a clean slate. No mistakes have been made; no history to dictate right or wrong to us. Like a fresh snowfall! Start anew. Create the right time for a new chapter in your life. Get excited about starting fresh.

Today is the perfect time to start a new chapter in your life!

18 January

Pay it forward. There was a story of a young lad who wanted to create a goodwill movement. He wanted to help three people with something they couldn't do themselves. The recipient could not return the favour but had to 'pay it forward' by helping three other people. Can you only imagine what a great place this would be if that were to happen all the time? It has to start somewhere. By helping three people and each of those people helping three people, you would very quickly be surrounded by kindness, generosity, warmth, and gratitude daily. What a wonderful world that would be.

Is this something we could try and practice pay it forward by helping others? The good feeling this would create would be phenomenal. And the more good feeling there is, the more we can pay it forward. Pay it forward today!

19 January

A wise, caring, and giving man was given £1,000 to hold onto until he found someone he felt needed it more than he. A few weeks passed. Then one day he was food shopping, and at the tills, a young mum was in front of him with four young children. She was managing really well, considering all four children were demanding a piece of her attention. The cashier gave the young women her bill, and the woman reached into her bag for her purse. No purse! Panic set in as bags of shopping sat waiting to be paid for, four kids were fussing, and a queue was building. The man held out his hand with an envelope containing the £1,000. "Here," he said, "please have this."

The woman, with tears in her eyes, said, "I woke up this morning and asked for a sign to stay. You see, my husband's job brought us here, and we know no one, I have no friends or family, his wages pay for the necessities, and we are miserable. Your generosity has proven prayers will be answered. Thank you!"

You never know what kind gesture, big or small, can change someone's life!

20 January

Today my thoughts are centred on expecting only the best and giving only the best. Today my mind and heart are open to new opportunities, and I will make the most out of every situation.

Today I will smile and act enthusiastically in everything I do. I will make every person I meet feel very important, and I will show them I care. Today my confidence is high, and I am willing to step out and take a chance. I will speak freely to all those I meet. I know I have something valuable to contribute. I expect results today, and my time is well invested.

Today I am one step closer to achieving my goals and dreams. I always keep my eyes focused on success and prosperity. Today I will sow good seeds so that I will reap my harvest of reward. Today is my day!

21 January

Do we find ourselves sometimes just going through the motions of our day-to-day lives? Do we ask ourselves sometimes, What if I had given everything? What if we make an effort to squeeze every opportunity out of our daily lives? Where would we be?

To make a stand can often be scary and it may hurt or wound us in some way, however, it may also be the best thing we ever do to change our lives and the loves around us for the better.

Try to give 100 percent in everything you do today!

22 January

I heard something interesting yesterday, "the Iceberg Analogy." If we take a cross-section of an iceberg, from the water level up, the iceberg is visible and tapers to a point. Underneath the water level, the iceberg gets bigger, wider, and deeper. The visible part of the iceberg represents behaviours in a person, his or her characteristics, and actions. The middle part just beneath the water's surface represents their beliefs. This often determines behaviour. The base of the iceberg, the strong, wide foundation, represents the values of a person.

Each section is needs to be present to form the iceberg, as are our behaviours, beliefs, and most important, values. Our values are what determine who we are. Be clear about your values, and know they are the solid foundation of who we are.

23 January

When others believe in us, when someone else believes in us, they see something that perhaps we don't. We are often too critical of ourselves and often self-sabotage our dreams. We hold an image in our minds of what we want to achieve. We find a way to reach it and in the same thought process, we find a reason or a way *not* to do it! We want others to believe in us, or at least it helps, as they often see more reasons why we should, could, and will achieve our dreams, and they encourage us further. I'd like to think we all have one person who believes in us. Ask the person why it is he or she believes in you to confirm we should believe in ourselves. I believe in you!

24 January

We don't need to look too far to find the beauty of our world brings us peace, calm, tranquillity, and the courage to go on.

Every life has its dark and cheerful times. Happiness comes from choosing which times to remember.

25 January

I think happiness should be bottled up and taken daily! There was an experiment done where a man stood on the street holding signs like "stressed," "tired," "aaaaagh," "angry," and so on. He attracted stressed, tired, and angry people to make comments and talk with him. He asked a few of them to join him for an hour or so, where he could have their attention. He spent time with them, talking with them about their lives and how they'd been feeling. They all agreed they had been moaning and feeling unhappy and negative. He switched the words they had been using, helped them feel better about where they were, and soon enough, the group felt and physically looked happier.

It's not going to happen overnight, but if we take a spoon of happiness daily, it's surely going to help. Better still, it's free! Be happy!

26 January

The father of a very wealthy family took his son on a trip to the country with the firm purpose to show him how poor people live. They spent a couple days and nights on a farm with a very poor family. "What did you learn about how poor people live, son?"

"I learnt that we have one dog; they have four. We have a pool that reaches to the middle of our garden, and they have a creek that has no end. We have imported lanterns in our garden, and they have the stars at night. We have a small piece of land to live on, and they have fields that go beyond our sight. We have servants; they serve others. We have walls around our property to protect; they have friends to protect them. We buy our food; they grow theirs." The father was speechless. "Thanks, Dad, for showing me how poor we are!"

27 January

When I woke up this morning, I wondered, *What is life all about, and what are some of the secrets of success in life?* The answers are right there in front of me, The roof said, "Aim high." The window said, "See the world." The clock said, "Every minute is precious." The mirror said, "Reflect before you act." The calendar said, "Be up to date." The door said, "Push hard for your goals," and my wardrobe said, "There is lots of opportunity."

And it's my choice. Carry a heart that always loves. Carry a touch that always heals. Carry a smile that lights others' lives.

28 January

If you want to love somebody, stand there and do it. If you don't, don't. There are no other choices. Live your life with no regrets. Be brave, and just choose.

30 January

There are always two sides, the good and the bad. The dark and the light, the sad and the glad. But in looking back over the good and the bad, we're aware of the number of good things we've had. And in counting our blessings, we find when we're through, we've no reason at all to complain or be blue. So be thankful for good things that have already been done, and feel grateful for the battles you've already won.

Helen Steiner Rice

It's always great to be reminded we've overcome so much. Be thankful and grateful today.

31 January

We all know there are lessons learnt every day. Probably one of the most common lessons we learn comes from how people behave or act. When someone performs an act of kindness, it makes us feel great, and we want to re-create it for someone else. However, when someone is unkind, it doesn't make us feel great, and we don't want to re-create it for someone else. Instead, we can use it as a lesson in how *not* to behave. Let's not get upset about it. Instead, just make sure we learn the lesson. However, when we witness someone behaving in a kind way, we can also use it as a lesson, especially when it creates a good feeling.

Make sure we use it as a lesson.

1 February

I've learned today that somebody's kind words can totally turn around your day.

A special friend told me she thought I was like my idol, Mary Kay Ash. To be even spoken about in the same sentence as Mary Kay Ash is an honour, let alone to be likened to her.

Never hold back kind words you may have to say to someone. You never know how they will affect the person or how they will make the individual feel. To speak kind words can be difficult at first, so why not make it our daily practice until it becomes a habit. Maybe even practice on ourselves, because only when we feel good, can we make others feel good.

I've learned today that somebody's kind words can totally turn around your life.

2 February

People are so very different, and all of us are amazing in our own right!

Someone very special to me, and to many others, shies away from any limelight or recognition. She is truly amazing in all she does as voluntary work for charities and schools. And she never asks for praise or recognition. In fact, when we do recognise her, it can sometimes be too much for her!

People like my friend amaze me and teach me so much about being humble and doing good just because, and for no other reason.

We all have different qualities. However, I think I will practice *this* today and do good just because, and for no other reason.

Have a humble day!

3 February

Why do people try to correct us if we don't fit in or feel unlike everyone else? Don't they realise they are breaking the mould of who we are meant to be. It is difficult enough when you don't fit in, without people trying to make you something you're not.

Why do we not embrace who we are and be proud of what makes us different? Some do! And some need guidance, reassurance, or courage to stand up and say, "I'm different, and I love it!"

We all have a purpose in life and a path to travel. Be sure *your* purpose and pathway are individual to you!

Be different in every way. It's what makes you exciting!

4 February

Wow! What a day we had yesterday. I have been awarded a pink car for achieving a certain level within my business. This pink car is bright pink, a really fun colour for a car.

On the school run in the morning, my daughter sat in the front, with the biggest grin on her face as people pointed and smiled at our pink car. The response we had was amazing. People smiled, pointed, and even took photos. All ages clearly enjoyed the colour.

The way people reacted surprised me. Do we really need something new and different to make us smile? Not necessarily, but the way it has made me feel is great. Smiles are infectious, and when people wave and smile at you, it feels great!

What can you use as your reason to smile today?

5 February

I heard this from a successful businessman who believes there are four types of people. Firstly, there are the people who always have to be right. They have a tendency to be narrow-minded and not very lenient, because they want to be right. Then there are people who are comfortable. If their houses were burning down around them, they would be comfy just where they were. There are people who just want to be liked by others and spend too much time worrying about what others think of them. And finally, there are those who like to win. They commit themselves fully and strive to be the best version of themselves they can be.

We all need a little bit of all four personalities, but mainly the last one, if we want to succeed in this tough world. Today, strive to be your best you!

6 February

How confused was I when I ordered a black coffee in a coffee house to be asked if I wanted regular, tall or grande, one shot or two; decaf or fully loaded; medium or rich roasted?

I replied, "Normal, straight up as it comes, no milk and no sugar. Please!"

She then asked, "Flavoured syrup?"

It got me thinking, *Do we overcomplicate our lives? Do we fill our lives with extra shots of frothy milk?* Admittedly, it's nice to have some variety, like a flavoured syrup on occasion. But if we overdo it, don't we miss out on enjoyment of the coffee? Enjoy what's important to you today normal, straight up, as it comes!

7 February

In times of uncertainty, we need to imagine we stand firmly on stable ground. If we can visualise our foundation as stable, we are likely to stand strong. If we imagine we stand on sand, we will always feel uncertain and, at times, wobbly.

Whatever is going on around us, it doesn't take much to knock us off our perch. So to know our base is strong and solid is enough to keep us going.

With clear knowledge of the past and a clear vision of the future, we can continue forward stronger and more prepared.

Stay strong and grounded as you travel through your days.

8 February

- They are hard working—Success takes hard work and those who are willing to do it.
- They are honest—Those who are successful long-term, are the honest ones.
- They persevere—How many success stories will go untold because they never happened? And all because someone quit. Successful people out last everybody else.
- They are friendly—Have you noticed that most successful people are friendly and people orientated?
- They arc lifo learners—Successful people are people who stretch themselves and grow continually, learning from all areas of life, including from their mistakes.
- They over-deliver—The old statement of under promise and over-deliver become famous because it made a lot of people successful.
- They seek solutions in the face of problems—Problems are opportunities to do the impossible not just complain. Successful people are the ones who find solutions.

Chris Widener

9 February

"If friends were flowers, I'd pick you and walk happily in my garden forever."

I love this saying as it says to us that we have a choice.

- We choose how we feel throughout our day.
- We choose to behave towards people in a way we would want to be treated.
- We choose what we think about.
- We love the choice!

And when we are surrounded by our choices, doesn't it make sense that we will be happy? Pick wisely, and walk happily forever.

10 February

"We don't know what we are capable of until we are given the opportunity."

I heard this yesterday, and it made me wonder, *What has appeared in our lives that we have had to deal with or overcome that we once thought we wouldn't be able to?*

We spend time worrying about what might happen and that we won't be able to cope or know what to do. And when we actually face that very situation, our only choice is to do what we once thought we weren't capable of.

Life has a funny way of dealing us the very things we need to grow. As a result, we gain skills, knowledge, and understanding that equip us to take on bigger and bigger challenges with confidence.

What are you capable of when given the opportunity?

11 February

Does your mind chatter drive you mad? Our mind chatter, also known as our crazies, is the voice in our head that talks us in and out of situations. We have positive thoughts in our minds and then they are spoilt by our mind chatter: "Don't be silly," "You're not brave enough," to name a few. Our mind chatter is like a fine garden; we can grow the most beautiful flowers, but if we don't tend to the weeds, they will eventually overtake the flowers. I believe if we learn to encourage and nurture the flowers (our loving and positive thoughts) and recognise which are weeds (our limiting and negative thoughts), our flowers will soon be the main focus in our gardens!

Have a day enjoying the flowers in your garden!

12 February

I'm sure we would all like to think we have grown personally. But what is personal development all about? We all have trials in our lives that test us, and we have overcome them *all* to get to where we are today.

Our personal development is measured by the size of our problems. The bigger our problems, the more we grow. Personal development is being bigger than your problems! So in a funny sort of way, we should feel grateful for big problems, as they are signs that we are growing.

That is something we can all get excited about.

13 February

"Less is more."

We all have our interpretations of this phrase, but I liked this one I heard the other day; The *less* you know, the *more* you learn, and the more you learn, the better you'll be.

Be happy knowing less, as it gives you the opportunity to learn more. The less you know the more you learn.

14 February

"One size fits all."

Not always. If there is anything I have learnt over the past few years, it is that it is so important for us to be adaptable. Being understanding and considerate to others is a must for us all to progress in this day and age. Learn about other people's personalities to get on with them better in a work environment as well as in a social place. The more we can adapt to others' personalities and styles, the better friend or business colleague we'll be. If we try and deal with all people and all situations in one way, I think we'll find one size does not fit all!

Learn to be adaptable to work with people better.

15 February

I was standing in my kitchen yesterday and noticed my orchid plant had the most amazing flowers on it. There were thirteen and three buds ready to burst. It was a truly beautiful plant in its height of glory. But the most amazing thing about this plant is that it was ready for the bin about three months ago. No flowers, the stems had become twig-like; there was no life in it at all.

When I told my friend about it, she said, "Cut it back, and give it a chance." I am so glad I did!

My orchid reminded me that sometimes when we are tired and have nothing else to give, we must give ourselves a chance. Go back to basics, and let nature take its course. Learn to trust that as long as you have belief the size of a mustard seed, you will be just fine.

16 February

"Girl power." This phrase was made famous by a girl group in the 1990s, but I think we underestimate the phrase in its true sense. You've probably heard the saying, "Women are like teabags; you don't know how strong they are until you drop them into hot water!" Never underestimate the power of a woman or similarly, a group of like-minded women. It's a fact that women share more with each other than men do with other men.

When a woman is put to the test, her natural beauty and confidence will surpass her tears if she lets it! A strong, confident woman who has a great state of mind makes a fantastic friend or partner.

Never underestimate the power of a woman.

17 February

We can sometimes think, *I need something to help me through,* or, *I need a miracle.* We all have obstacles placed in our way or go through stormy times. It's not the absence of the storm that makes us different; it's who we discover in the storm. In other words, it's not what our lives look like now but how we've grown to this day.

We sometimes look elsewhere for answers, seek someone else's help, when all the time the answers are within *us.* We can take on the roles of many different people if we just trust all we've learnt.

Every day we are challenged to grow. Discover more about you and all you have become through your stormy times. You have all you need to be the most amazing you.

18 February

Careful planning avoids poor performance. It's amazing how taking a few minutes at the start of each day to plan and set your thoughts in the right direction can help you get ahead and empower you to accomplish so much. Too often we get caught up in the activity of life and tend to just go with the flow. When it comes to your life, you should be setting the flow.

Of course, unexpected things happen. Our days won't always go according to plan. We need to be flexible, and if we take time each day to set our hearts and minds in the right direction, we'll be equipped for whatever comes our way.

19 February

My little man, seven-year-old Jodi, goes to sleep each night listening to music. He has a song he puts on repeat, so it plays constantly for a few hours. I turn it off when I go to sleep.

Why do I leave it playing even when he is asleep? Because I believe he can hear the lyrics while he's sleeping. The song is titled "You Are Amazing."

If you asked Jodi how he was during the day, he would say, "Amazing." If he was playing a game, he would clench his fist and say, "I'm amazing." If you asked him how he played in his football game, he'd say, "Amazing!" There is definitely something to be said for feeding your brain while you are asleep.

You are amazing!

20 February

Somewhere over the rainbow,
Way up high,
There's a land that I heard of
once in a lullaby.
Somewhere over the rainbow,
Skies are blue.
And the dreams that you dare to dream
Really do come true . . .
If happy little bluebirds fly above the rainbow,
Why, oh why can't I?

Harold Arlen

I love this song! I think it tells us there is somewhere we can go and be whoever we want to be. I think it tells us this somewhere is where only dreams come true! No dreams, no entry! Somewhere we can go where our dreams become reality.

This place can exist, but only if we believe it does. See you somewhere over the rainbow!

21 February

It only takes the smallest adjustment to make a difference. We rearranged the furniture in our lounge earlier. We fiddled until we got to a stage where we had to leave it or go mad. Did we need to buy an extra piece of furniture? Did we need less furniture? Had we started something that was going to escalate out of control? My dad popped 'round as we were finishing. Believe it or not, all we did was turn one of the chairs a few inches to change the whole dynamics of the room.

We sometimes think drastic changes need to be made to make a difference, but all it really takes is tiny adjustment to give us a different result. Sometimes, the simplest of tweaks can be all that is needed to make the biggest difference.

22 February

Food for thought today. Without olives being squeezed, there would be no olive oil. Without grapes being pressed, there would be no wine. Without the dough being kneaded, bread wouldn't rise. So if you are feeling a little under pressure, don't worry. A little pressure is what's needed to bring out the best in you! I love this thought as it reminds us it is OK to feel a little overwhelmed or under pressure at times. It is in times like these that we learn the most about ourselves and what our capabilities are.

So if you are feeling a little under pressure, don't worry. A little pressure is what's needed to bring out the best in you!

23 February

My daughter has a cushion on her bed that says, "Always kiss me goodnight." I love this pillow, as it reminds me to always kiss her goodnight, and whisper to her how special she is and how much I love her. She stays asleep as I tell her what I want her to know.

One morning she said to me she dreamt what I had said to her the night before. How powerful is that? What are we telling ourselves the last thing at night? Are we clearing our minds of rubbish and replacing it with what we love about ourselves? It truly works and has a profound effect on our state of mind in the morning.

Give it a go, and tell yourself how wonderful you are before you go to sleep.

24 February

Today I am giving you a daily survival kit.

- Toothpick—Pick the good qualities in everyone, including yourself.
- Rubber band—Be flexible; things might not always go the way you want, but it can be worked out.
- Plaster—Heal hurt feelings, either yours or someone else's.
- Eraser—We all make mistakes. That's OK; we learn by our errors.
- Mint—You are worth a mint to your family.
- Bubble gum—Stick with it, and you can accomplish anything.
- Pencil—List your blessings every day.
- Teabag—Relax daily, and go over that list of your blessings.

Wishing you love, gratitude, friends, and laughter.

25 February

- The tendency to act and think spontaneously.
- Unmistakable ability to enjoy every moment.
- Loss of interest of judging other people.
- Loss of interest in interpretation/explaining the actions of others.
- Loss of interest in conflict.
- Loss of the ability to worry.
- Experience frequent episodes of appreciation and contented feelings of connectedness with others and nature.
- Frequent attacks of smiling. [I love this one!]
- Increase acceptance of love given by others and the uncontrollable urge to extend it.

Peace Pilgrim

I wish you inner peace.

26 February

How to stay young.

- Keep only cheerful friends.
- Keep learning.
- Enjoy the simple things.
- Laugh often, long and loud!
- The tears happen, so endure, grieve, and move on.
- Surround yourself with what you love.
- Cherish your health.
- Don't take guilt trips.
- Tell people you love them at every opportunity.

Life is not measured by the breaths we take but by the moments that take your breath away.

27 February

There are wonderful things prepared for our future! Even though we might be facing some circumstances that seem unfair, or things aren't going the way we planned, our good plan still remains.

Remember, in order to keep our lives moving in the right direction, we need to keep our thoughts, heart, and words moving in the right direction. When we start recounting all our blessings and the good things in our lives, we'll find we are blessed beyond what we could ever imagine.

Right now, take a moment and think about all the goodness in our lives. Focus on all that is good. Keep our words and thoughts going in the right direction, so we can keep moving forward into the abundant life ahead of us!

Focusing on all the goodness is what completely changed my life!

28 February

Something I heard today got me thinking, *Life is a patchwork!*

I like the idea of life represented by a patchwork quilt. What would your patches represent?

I thought mine could represent

Emotions	Health	Fun	Friendships	Feelings	Belief	Love
Compassion	Wealth	Trust	Determination	Family	Faith	Imagination
Freedom	Colour	Hope	Relationships	Energy . . .	always	Energy!

Those are just some of my patches. What about yours?

Have fun with your quilt!

29 February

What inspires you? Is it someone you love? Is it a piece of music, a book, a film? Things and people inspire us daily; we just don't always notice them. I truly wish you have something, some words or a story within this book, to help inspire you.

Spend a moment each day to find what inspires us, ticks our box so we then have the drive to commit to our dreams. We can't do it all on our own, and it makes sense to seek help from wherever we can. Inspiration comes in all shapes, sizes, ages, and forms. And it often comes when it is least expected.

Be inspired, stay inspired, and be inspiring

1 March

From a distance, two horses look like each other. But if you look closely, you'll notice one of the horses is blind. If you stand nearby and listen, you will hear the sound of a bell and see it comes from the smaller horse in the field. It lets the blind friend know where it is, so it can follow. The horse with the bell checks that the blind horse heard him. The blind horse listens for the bell and then slowly follows, trusting it will not be led astray.

Like the owners of these two horses, we are not thrown away just because we are not perfect or because we have problems or challenges. Sometimes, we are the blind horse, being guided by the ringing bell of those placed in our lives. Other times, we are the guide horse, helping others find their way.

I wish you friends with bells when you need them.

2 March

I'm sure we've all wondered, *If I were financially secure, that I have enough money to take care of my needs now and in the future, how would I live my life? Would I change anything?* We need to let ourselves go and not hold back on our dreams. Describe a life that is complete and richly yours. Have we ever stopped and actually asked ourselves, "If," and actually written it down "as if" it were now? How powerful could this be?

It's very important to speak in the now: "I am," "I have," "I enjoy," and so on. We know all thoughts are energy. Using language in the present tense keeps our thought process moving in the right direction and start to create our ideal lives "as if" it were true.

Imagine, how would you live your life?

3 March

Someone asked what motivates me? The million dollar question!

Could you give an answer in one sentence? Very quickly I answered, "The first thing that motivates me is my adorable children. As a mum, I am a role model to my kids, and if I want them to achieve, I want to lead by example!"

My friend said, "It's just that you are always so upbeat, happy, and focused."

My first thought was, *Why not?* I truly believe it's a choice to drip feed ourselves with motivation. It's all too easy to not bother. Then the spiral downward is all too slippery. We can occasionally find it harder to stay motivated, but it sure is fun when it works. Build the momentum, and it becomes easier.

The easier it becomes, the happier you will be.

4 March

Treasure who is important to you! When a devoted father and avid art collector lost his beloved son, he was devastated. The father's favourite painting was one of his son a friend painted. It had pride of place in his house. After the father died, his paintings were auctioned, including the one of his son, all estimated worth millions of pounds.

The first painting auctioned was the painting of his son. No one wanted it. The buyers insisted the valuable paintings be shown. The man's gardener came forward and bid for the painting of the son, as he, too, was a devoted father. He loved the man dearly, and knowing how precious the painting was to the father, he was pleased to have won it for a nominal fee. The instructions were whoever wanted the painting of his son inherited the whole estate and paintings.

Treasure who is important to you!

5 March

My little man arrived home with a friend after a party. I hadn't seen him before he went, and I was pleasantly surprised to see he wore his best clothes. Age seven, Jodi wore his smart, black jeans; his best shirt and tie, and his matching waistcoat; and the new boots his dad bought him for a roller disco. After giving him a loving hug, I double-checked he had been a good boy and was told he was, "a lovely little boy," and, "a real credit," to us.

I was, however, intrigued as to his choice in attire. I asked, "Is there any reason you wore your best clothes to the party, Jodi?" He explained there was a little girl in his class, whom he liked; in his words, he "loved her." I asked, "Why do you love her?"

He said, "Because she smiles a big smile, which makes her pretty, and we have fun." How amazing it is for him to know that at just seven years old.

Do you notice the simplest of things that your loved ones do?

6 March

Time to shine. Do you ever feel you would like to have a moment to shine?

Create a moment for you to shine. No one needs know, but it will sure make you feel good. When you shine, you light the way for others to do the same. Liberty, my ten-year-old daughter, had an audition for a production at a well-known theatre. The director brought her out, said she was amazing, and he would like her to come back for another audition. She just shone. I think Liberty enjoyed her shining moment! Shining moments are infectious and definitely make you and others feel great. Liberty was on cloud 9 all day.

Have a shining moment for yourself, and light the way for others.

7 March

The specific events in our lives are not as significant as our progressive capacity to learn from them. Some of our ideas may not be the right ones but they give us inspiration and direction from which to develop better ideas.

We should indeed defend our beliefs but take care that our defences are not the walls of a dungeon, keeping us trapped and out of reach of new light. We learn most when considering precisely where we may be wrong. When one of our ideas is proved wrong we should rejoice that a new growing point has appeared. We are more likely to learn from opponents than sycophants. Popular acclaim is risky, more likely to lead to stagnation and decline than individuality and creativity. Although occasional support and encouragement are refreshing, ultimately our individual journeys are exclusively our own.

There is no better goal than to be happy to be alive each day, full of wonder, enthusiasm and gratitude for further opportunity to grow.

Robert Lefever, *Life Is a Journey,* 1998

8 March

Desire. What is desire? Desire is what tugs on your shirt tails and says, "You can do this." You wouldn't have a burning desire if you weren't able. Desire is what gets us up and going.

D   Determination—We need it to carry us through.

E   Energy—It goes without saying, we need energy!

S   Spirit—We have to have spirit; it's what makes us unique.

I   Inspiration—Always!

R   Remind ourselves why we want something.

E   Express yourself and enjoy.

Desire can mean different things to different people. What is your desire?

9 March

I was spreading butter on toast this morning with a teaspoon, because all the knives were in the dishwasher. I didn't think it would matter. How wrong was I! I was making more work for myself and ended up with lumpy butter and torn toast. It still tasted the same. But it didn't look great, and it took me a lot longer to spread the butter.

Do we sometimes make more work for ourselves by using the wrong tools? Tools, meaning physical things but also our minds. Do we mean well only to have our attitude trip us up? How much more efficient would we be if we were more organised and made sure we used a knife to spread our butter, and if our toolkits were well equipped to cope with any job that comes our way?

May you always have a knife handy to spread your butter!

10 March

How do you feel? Do you feel frustrated and that there's not enough time? Or do you feel you are patient, and there is enough time to explore possibilities? When we feel frustrated, we feel tense, frazzled, a bit restless, easy to anger, and tired. Those are just some of the feelings. When we feel at peace, we feel calm, generous, respectful, appreciative and like we have all the time in the world. Which feelings do you want to experience?

Did you know that feeling peaceful is a real beauty secret? It makes your appearance more soft and approachable. The more peaceful you are, the more attractive you'll be.

We now have no excuse but to look great every day. Be peaceful to stay young and calm.

11 March

How deep is your pain? I'm sure most of us have experienced some sort of pain. Our perception of pain can differ each time. Experiencing huge amounts of pain or consistent amounts of pain, means it can become deep-rooted. Over time, we may feel we have dealt with our pain. But then something may trigger it, and all our emotions and feelings related to the pain return, and we relive it.

Is it possible pain is an illusion? Can it be something that we make into an illusion, so it becomes no longer a part of us? When we can deal with it and hand it over. We can change our perception of pain, so it no longer lives deep within us; it can no longer stop us from progressing. We can visit it, but then keep ourselves removed from it.

Face the illusion of pain and free yourself to enable you to enjoy your life now!

12 March

Do you fit in? No? Great! I spent the afternoon with my business colleagues, sharing stories about our childhood experiences. We were all pleasantly surprised we had similar stories. As a child at school, we had only a couple of good friends, we were quiet, and kept ourselves to ourselves. One of us found it hard to speak up and stand up for herself. Some of us were the ones picked last for gym. You can picture what it was like for us. We just didn't fit in and had little confidence. Sound familiar?

Now look at us. We all have very successful businesses, are lucky to have an abundance of great friends, regularly speak in public, and inspire and motivate others to make the most of their lives. You could say our childhood adversities shaped the wonderful lives we have today. So by not fitting in as a child, we had to work to overcome life's little challenges. Or you could say we had the profile of an entrepreneur!

13 March

Improvise with what you have. I witnessed a birthday present being given, and it was wrapped with clear plasters. The girl giving the present said she had run out of sticky tape, and plasters were all she had. I loved it. For me, the present was still presented gift-wrapped, thought had gone into it, and she made the most of what she had and improvised.

Let's face it, the paper was only going in the bin! Sometimes we don't get started with projects, because we don't have the right tools, or it's not the right time. I think this present is a perfect example of getting started with what you have and improvise!

Make the most with what you have.

14 March

Drip-feed yourself with positivity! We know that to be positive rather than negative is the way forward. However, in our busy day-to-day life, we can sometimes lose sight of the positive things in our lives. I placed a dozen or so little smiley face stickers around my home. Each time we see one, we have to think of something positive. For example, "I am having a fabulous day," or, "I am very lucky to be so fortunate!" You can be as specific as you want, but it is important it's positive! It could simply be, "I love the sunshine."

This has a remarkable effect on our thought process and keeps the positivity constant. Regular injections of positive affirmations change our day. Try it for yourself and see!

Drip-feed yourself with positivity, and see your world change!

15 March

If you want to climb great heights, your legs and arms have to work together.

It is no good having a dream, a goal, and an aspiration if you are not prepared to work at it or if you have a defeatist attitude. It would be like having your foot on the accelerator and the brake at the same time; nothing would happen. Everything has to work in harmony. Fix your sights on where you are going or what you want to achieve, apply your physical body, and get your mind in gear, and there is no stopping you. If you have a destination in mind with no fixed plan of how to get there, you could end up going backwards.

Focus on great heights, and great heights you will climb.

16 March

Water flows into the Dead Sea from the River Jordan. It does not flow out anywhere, as the Dead Sea is far below the main sea level. There are no outlet streams. It is estimated that over a million tons of water evaporate from the Dead Sea every day, leaving it salty, too full of minerals, and unfit for marine life.

Think about it. If we take and do not give back, how is it possible for good things to live in us? If we get a Dead Sea mentality, taking in more water, more money, more everything without giving anything back, the results aren't good.

Make sure you have outlets in the sea of your own life. Many outlets for love, wealth, and all things wonderful in your life. Make sure you don't just get; you give, too. Open the taps, and you'll open the floodgates to happiness.

Make it a habit to share, to give.

17 March

Brave and calm in the face of adversity. I met a woman earlier today who, on my first impression, was very friendly, smiley, chatty, and professional. I warmed to her straight away. After a few hours, it became apparent she and her family were in the middle of a crisis. Their home was to be demolished in two weeks.

You would have never known she was facing such a difficult time. She remained professional and didn't let her feelings affect her work. "What's the point in getting worked up. It won't achieve anything, apart from insanity!" What a great way to be; how brave and calm she is.

You never know what battle one is facing, so give people a chance. Stay brave and calm in the face of adversity, and you are unlikely to lose your mind.

18 March

Your gut feeling is an incredibly accurate thing. It is rarely wrong. We talk about a gut feeling, something we feel in our core. Your head can see or feel one thing, and very often you feel something different in your core. Your gut feeling can often go against logic and all rationalisation, making it sometimes difficult to follow. It's easier to let our heads rule rather than slow down and concentrate on our gut feeling.

My gut feeling has never let me down, so I now know to trust it. I think we can underestimate our bodies and what they try to tell us. I, for one, have spent time to recognise what my body is trying to tell me.

Get in tune with your whole self, and let your body do the talking.

19 March

While I sat in the doctor's surgery with my daughter, I was reminded of how unmotivating it is to be surrounded by moaning and groaning people. Why is it people try and outdo each other with their ailments? "Oh dear, that's terrible. I've had the same problem and—"

"Oh, you think that's bad, my husband has . . ." I was relieved when we were called in and could escape the negativity of the waiting room.

It is so important to surround yourself with positive people. Like attracts like. What you think about you will attract others who think the same. Never underestimate your surroundings. If you want to be happy, be happy. It is as simple as that!

20 March

A friend shared a horrifying experience with me. A few days before, she was mugged by two men. With a dislocated arm she lay hurt, screaming for help. When the men fled, she remembers people coming to her aid. One woman noted the registration of the car the men drove away in, while others helped my friend to her feet. She still had hold of her car keys so was able to get home. My friend was distraught, asking, "Why me?"

The muggers' car was found, with the men and all the bags they had stolen. My friend was relieved and soon realised she was attacked so all the other people could get their belongings back. As she said, they picked on the wrong person. How amazing and what a great way to look at such a horrifying experience!

Everything in this world happens for a reason.

21 March

Are you lucky enough to be doing the work you love? Or are you going through the motions of going to work, turning out a day, and receiving your pay cheque at the end of the month?

I, fortunately, am in the first group, enjoying my work, loving what I do, and surrounded by others who feel the same. Isn't it a shame when people don't enjoy what they do? However, there are ways to make it better. Remind yourself that whatever you do, you are making a difference. Otherwise, it wouldn't be called work. Make the most out of the people you work with, build relationships, get to know your colleagues better. You never know what you may have in common. If you are lucky to enjoy what you do, carry on doing a great job; you are really making a difference.

22 March

Life lives in words! Have you ever paid great attention to the words you speak? They have a massive impact on your life and how your daily routine pans out.

One experiment which has a highly effective result is to wear an elastic band around one wrist. Each time you find yourself saying something negative, for example, "I can't do it," "it's too expensive," "that's impossible," pick the band away from the wrist and let go. This leaves a flicking, and sometimes painful feeling on the wrist.

The purpose is to remind you that something has to change within your language to adapt your way of thinking. After a short while, you'll be surprised what a difference it makes. Highly effective and easy to do.

Life lives in words!

23 March

Enthusiasm is infectious! We all know that like attracts like, good or bad. It only takes one person to be fired up to inject others with enthusiasm. Everyone can be enthusiastic; all it takes are excitement and passion, along with energy. Enthusiasm is easy to catch and easy to pass on! When someone shares his or her enthusiasm with you, take it and pass it on. When people share in your enthusiasm, it will also reaffirm your excitement for your purpose and encourage you to go further. Be enthusiastic and act enthusiastically, and you will become enthusiastic.

Be enthusiastic, and you will attract so many others. Enthusiasm is infectious!

24 March

You can't take it back. Two children were asked to conduct an experiment and teach the rest of the class a lesson. One child was asked to squeeze all the toothpaste out of the tube onto a plate. The second was asked to put the toothpaste back in the tube. She was unable to do so. The teacher asked what they thought the lesson might be. The first child explained that if you imagine the toothpaste represents words, once you've said something, you can't take it back. I thought this was an excellent way to bring two feuding friends together and use props to show the importance of being aware of the words you speak.

Choose how you act, and speak carefully. Just like the toothpaste, you can't take it back.

25 March

If it doesn't feel right, stop and adjust it. I'm sure many of us have done it—bought a shirt, tried it on, and it fits perfectly, except the collar feels slightly uncomfortable. You then realise you left the cardboard in the collar. To fix it, simply take the cardboard out, and your collar is comfortable enough to wear.

Too many times we carry on in our daily lives with things that niggle us, whether people or circumstances. It doesn't feel right, but because we may not know exactly what the problem is, we don't know how or what to change.

Stay in tune with yourself. And when something doesn't feel right, stop and adjust it. You are likely to function a lot better if you do.

26 March

Do we realise how amazing we are? I was sat in the physiotherapy clinic, studying the posters on the wall, fascinated by the human body and how it works. We have hundreds of muscles, and they are only part of the functioning body. We truly are a miracle, and I'm not sure we appreciate how amazing we are. Our bodies have the ability to do so much more than we ask it to do, so why do we not use it to its full potential? Why do we think our bodies are not capable? Is it because we are not aware of how the mechanics of our minds and our matter work in harmony? We say babies are miracles, so what changes?

Realise how amazing you are.

27 March

Earlier in the week, I rang a colleague, and her teenage daughter answered her phone. She had to walk a couple of minutes to her mum to pass the phone. I have never met the daughter, and to my delight, this little voice asked, "So how are you today? Are you enjoying the sunshine?" Some teenagers can be short of conversation, but we had a lovely chat.

Later that evening, a client of my husband's called the home phone. I have never met this lady, and because Brian wasn't in, she started up a fascinating conversation.

I put down the phone, thinking how lovely it was there are still people out there who, like me, love to chat and are interested in other people.

Take time today to chat to someone new to you or someone you would like to know more about. It's very refreshing.

28 March

Even though we may not know it, we are teachers. Teachers to our friends and our families. If we are parents, then to our children. We teach others with what we say. We teach others with what we do and how we behave. As teachers, we plant the seed and help water it. The rest is up to others to nurture and to grow. We teach by example. We walk the walk and talk the talk. We must try not to judge and show love instead. To show compassion and be compassionate is an important quality, and one we should practice often. Are we men and women of our word? Remember, you are a teacher.

29 March

Money can be a difficult subject. A wise man once told me money was energy doesn't like to be hoarded. It is important for money to flow, flow in and flow out. Not all in or all out but to learn how to use it to our advantage. We've heard the saying, "You need to spend money to make money," meaning be generous rather than hoard it.

Give where you can, and you will always be paid back in abundance. Don't be frightened to accept money coming your way. Money doesn't care where it goes. Respect money, and it stays with you; disrespect it, and it will shy away from you. I know it may sound silly, but an abundance of money is a state of mind. Too many people focus on debt and lack of money rather than on prosperity and an abundance of money.

Money doesn't care where it goes. Respect it, and it stays with you.

30 March

I have been working with women lately and have asked them to share with me their whys. Why do they get up in the morning? Why are you focused on a particular thing?

Hearing other people's purposes highlights for me that we are all different. What floats one person's boat would not float the next person's.

Then why do we think treating people the same way is going to help them or us? We need to be understood so that those around us can get the best out of us. We need to be more specific with what we communicate the others.

Be clear in your mind what your "why" is, and be aware that your "why" may not be the same as the next person's.

Isn't that what makes the world go around?

31 March

Do you ever lose yourself in the moment? The intensity of what has your attention makes you feel you are the only one in the world.

We watched a concert recently, and the lead singer was in that place. Not only was he consumed in his performance, he had us captivated as well. Now that is losing yourself in the moment if you can take others with you.

It's a very comforting feeling when you can shut everything else out and totally enjoy your moment. We often find we are reenergised and filled to overflowing.

It is more often something we are extremely passionate about that can take us to that place. Lose yourself in the moment occasionally. It's a great place to be.

1 April

Smiling is contagious and free!

Have a think about what makes you smile. Is it spending time with family and friends? Is it the sun shining through your curtains in the morning? Is it seeing two people in an embrace who clearly care for each other? Similarly, what makes you laugh? I once heard laughing described as jogging on the inside. I make it my purpose to smile at one new person each day. You never know whose day you will brighten.

Kids are the best examples of this. One summer, our daughter, who was six at the time, made friends with a foreign little girl. They played for hours every day. I asked Liberty, "What's your friend's name?"

She said, "I don't know. She speaks another language I don't understand." Then she said, "Mummy, we don't need to understand what each other is saying, as a smile is the same in any language." How true. This was a lesson re learnt, and that she does pay attention to me at home and had smiled at her little friend to be understood.

Don't forget to smile!!

2 April

"Don't worry; be happy." A great saying and a great song, but do we really understand its intention? We do have a tendency to worry which stops us from being happy.

When we worry, our face frowns. Believe it or not, that is harder work for our muscles in our face than smiling. Other people are not drawn to a frowning face. But they *are* attracted to a happy, smiling face. Make it our daily purpose to think, if only for a short while, about what makes us happy. Amazingly, you will find other people are happy back.

Happiness is like sunshine on a rainy day. Where will you let your sun shine? Who can you be a ray of sunshine to? Be happy today!

3 April

Are you reading the wrong map? If we embark on a journey we have never made before, we are often guided by a map or a satnav device to get us there. Interestingly enough, don't you enjoy the journey more when it is all planned out before you begin? If we get in the car with no destination in mind, we would drive around aimlessly, wasting time! Equally, if we have an incorrect address to follow, we will not reach our correct destination. We have to be specific on where we are going. Otherwise, it is a waste of time! I once heard it described, "You will never get a chocolate cake from a meat loaf recipe!"

Decide on your destination, and plan your route. The route may change along the way, but you will always arrive if you have a destination in mind!

4 April

Yesterday was my birthday, and I had the most amazing day. Firstly, I was surprised by my ten-year-old daughter, who had decorated the lounge with balloons and bought flowers and cupcakes with her own money to decorate the dining-room table. I was so spoilt with treats and messages of best wishes from family and friends. The kids took great pleasure in writing the most beautiful messages in my cards. I spent the whole day being fussed over. I had so much fun it will be a birthday I will remember for a very long time.

Do we fuss over the ones we love often enough? Do we show them how important they are to us? I felt like a million dollars. I would definitely want to make others feel the same. Do we make it our daily practice to make others feel important?

5 April

If you could liken your body and being to a building, what would you be? Would you be a greenhouse made of glass, fragile and easily broken? Or are you a cathedral, strong and beautiful, grand, and a place where all are welcome? Is the foundation of your building strong and built on solid ground? If your bricks could represent anything, what would that be? Would they represent love, hope, or pride? Or maybe doubt, fear, or even forgiveness, light, or energy? The list is endless. What is the state of your building? What can be done to improve it? Use more positive bricks? Invite more people in to share your building? Most importantly, is it all held together with love?

Build your building wide, deep, and strong and with love and passion.

6 April

Who do we turn to in times of need? Is it your higher power? A friend or family member? A colleague? We choose someone who is going to support us, someone we respect and love to help us make the right decisions. Someone who will guide us in the right direction and hold our hand, if need be.

Could we be that person for someone else? It works both ways. We may have to be the guide and support for someone else. We often call on others for support and advice, but do we allow ourselves to be the one to offer guidance and support? When we share our ideas with others, it helps us, too.

Let's be aware that even though we may need others, we are also available for support and guidance for them. Show them we are caring and open-minded, and that we want to help.

7 April

My amazing daughter has just turned to me and said, "I've got something for your *Butterfly Whispers*, Mummy. You can't score a goal if you don't take a shot." Don't you just love how a child's mind works? It got me thinking. In order to score a goal, say in football, you have to possess the ball, and to have the ball, a team member has to see you are available to accept a pass.

What does your team look like, and who do you have around you? Teaming up with and having nourishment from others help us work through life's challenges. With a varied and positive team of people around you, you can take a shot at the goal and score!

8 April

I was driving home from church this morning, and traffic came to a standstill as hundreds of runners crossed the road. They were taking part in our local 10 km race. On this gorgeous sunny morning, these runners had taken time out to run and raise money for charity. As I waited, I watched as these men and women of all ages, shapes, and sizes ran past me towards their finishing line. Every runner was different. Some had big stride patterns, some had awkward running styles, some looked happy, and some looked as though they'd had enough. But all were going in the same direction. It didn't matter how they got there; it just mattered that they finished. Then I saw a man tied to a woman's arm. On the back of her bib it said, "blind runner." Amazing!

However different we all are, each of us is running our own race. And whatever your style is, it's your unique style. Keep running! You're doing a great job!

9 April

Pain is temporary. It may last a minute, an hour, a day, a year, but eventually it will subside and something else will take its place. If I quit, however, it lasts forever.

Lance Armstrong

Pain is so different for so many different people. Pain has many levels.

Much of our pain is inevitable and happens as we grow through life. It's what makes us who we are. However, there are some levels of pain which are not expected and truly test our limits. But if we can just hold in our minds Armstrong's quote and know the pain will subside, we are likely to cope a lot better with immediate pain. If we let the pain take us over, it will, however, last forever.

Let go of the pain you hold. Try to replace it with something wonderful in your life. Pain will not exist when there is delight. Remember, pain is temporary!

10 April

If the mountain is smooth, how are you going to climb it?

When you put it like that, it seems obvious we need little bumps along our climb to make it easier to reach the top. We know how hard it would be to climb a mountain of ice. But if we throw a few patches of snow and rock in our way, the mountain would be a lot easier to climb.

Imagine the patches of snow and rock as our challenges and struggles in life, and see them as stepping stones on our mountain climb. They somehow are now bearable or even welcome. It would be near impossible to climb a mountain of ice, smooth and slippery.

So welcome your challenges and struggles as a helping hand along your mountain climb. If the mountain were smooth, how could you climb it?

11 April

Since having children, it's occurred to me that we ask them to be brave and to stand for what they believe in. But do we? Is it because we have too many fears? Fears we have collected over the years. The two fears we are born with are fear of loud noises and fear of falling.

When we step out of our comfort zone we grow as a person. I make it my daily purpose to give an extra 10 percent in all I do throughout the day, work or play and to go the extra mile. If we continue to do what's familiar, it's maintenance, and we move along at a steady pace. If you continually give a little extra, step out from what is familiar and do something every so often that scares you, you'll be surprised. Try it! It's a great feeling of accomplishment.

Step out of your comfort zone today.

12 April

How to have the tallest building in town? To be the tallest building in town is not to be bigger or better than anyone else but to be the best or tallest *you* can be! Concentrate on building tall, brick by brick, day by day. Spend time on your own personal development, and be aware of the lessons to be learnt every day.

Some people believe the only way to have the tallest building is to knock down other people's buildings by criticising, finding fault, and metaphorically pulling down their buildings. Visualise the skyline. It's going to look spectacular if we help build each other's buildings. It's the law of life; if we help others build their buildings with love and support, ours, too, will build quicker.

How are you going to have the tallest building in town?

13 April

I watched *Nanny McPhee* with the children at the cinema today. Nanny McPhee is a truly odd-looking character, with warts 'n all! She was employed to look after five unruly and naughty children. She had five lessons to teach them.

1. Stop fighting.
2. Learn to share.
3. Help each another.
4. Be brave.
5. Have faith.

Each time the children learnt one of the lessons, one of her warts disappeared, or her nose became smaller. After a while, Nanny McPhee became a beautiful woman, as all her warts disappeared.

If we practice daily these five lessons, we, too, metaphorically become better looking and enjoyable to be around.

14 April

The bamboo plant. For years, the farmer waters the seeds of his bamboo plant with no evidence of growth. The bamboo seeds grow roots underground, with no signs above ground for about five years. Some seeds never grow roots, but the farmer won't know for years but waters them anyway. After years of growing roots under the surface, the plant experiences an incredible growth spurt and becomes the tallest plant in the jungle.

I love this analogy, as it represents personal development. We sometimes have to put the work in before we see any change, and it can be frustrating. Keep watering your roots, have faith, believe in yourself, and your growth is inevitable.

You will be the tallest plant in your jungle.

15 April

Have faith in your dreams! My parents always taught me I could do anything I wanted if I believed in myself and was prepared to work for it. I have always believed this to be true! Have a clear idea of what you want to do and what makes you happy. Dedicate your energies to its pursuit, and there is no knowing what you can achieve, particularly if others are inspired by your dream and offer to help. I liken having faith in your dreams to a bungee jump. We can all stand at the top of a cliff, but the one who has faith in his or her dreams is the one who jumps, knowing there is a rope tied to their ankles. Jumping is not always an easy decision to make but a necessary one if you want your dreams to become reality.

"When you follow your dreams, your soul must be with you" (Liberty, age Ten.

16 April

Let your inner beauty shine! Inner beauty is something we all have.

People are like stained-glass windows, an ordinary window until the sun shines through them. Our true beauty is only revealed when there is a light from within. When we concentrate on our strengths and are tuned into our uniqueness, that is when our light shines through.

Look inside for your strengths, and your inner beauty will shine through.

We can all be as different and as beautiful as a stained-glass window for all to see!

17 April

Say, "Thank you." We love hearing, "Thank you," don't we? It should be our daily practice to say, "Thank you," to express our appreciation sincerely and without the expectation of anything in return. Truly appreciate the people around you, and you will soon find more appreciative people around you. Truly appreciate life, and you will find you have more good things come your way. Have an attitude of gratitude! Don't just say, "Thank you," for a birthday present or a door held open for you. Say, "Thank you," for blue sky or another person's smile!

Thank you for reading this message today!

18 April

It's all about how we feel and how we make others feel. Everyone likes to be made to feel special, so make it your daily purpose to imagine everyone with a sign around their necks saying, "Make me feel important." It's amazing how much better it makes you feel.

I once heard a quote by Maya Angelou, "People will forget what you said, they will forget what you did, but they will never forget how you made them *feel.*" Feelings are everything!

What you send out into the lives of others really does come back into your own. Make others feel special, and you will feel special, too.

19 April

Time
Take time to work, for it is the price of success.
Take time to think, it is the source of strength.
Take time to play, it is the secret of youth.
Take time to read, it is the seed of wisdom.
Take time to be friendly, for it brings happiness.
Take time to dream, for it will take you to the stars.
Take time to love, it is the joy of life.
Take the time to be content, it is the music of the soul.

—Russell Museum

20 April

We've all failed at something, however big or small, and overcome it. So we can do it again! Life is all about learning from our mistakes. The beauty of it is that no matter how many times we fail, there is always another chance. Failure is not falling down; it's staying down. Let's change the word 'failure' to '*fallure*'! When small children fall, we dust them down and encourage them to carry on, because we don't want them to be frightened of falling and to toughen them up.

Treat yourself like a child next time you fall down. "There, there, dust yourself down, and carry on!" Don't be frightened of fallure! Get excited about the fact you get to give it another go!

21 April

It's all too easy to find fault in ourselves. It's too easy to remember what we are not very good at or how we have failed in some way. Get to know yourself better, and focus on your strengths. For some, this may be tricky, so ask a few people who love you dearly what makes you special and unique. It may be your smile or your cooking. You may be an amazing singer or have the ability to make people laugh.

We all have talents and are unique in our own ways. We may just not see it! Repeat to yourself what others find special about you, and see yourself through their eyes. In the mirror we can focus on what we don't like about ourselves. Change your mindset, and see yourself as a new you!

22 April

Added value! The kids and I sat on a ride at the fun fair, ready for an adventure. Little did we realise it was a ride for little ones. After we went around in a small circle, we all looked at each other as if to ask, "Is that it?" Half the ride was in a tunnel, and half was outside. The man controlling the ride was dressed like a pirate and wearing a big grin. He knew what was coming next. He leapt onto the ride and sprayed everyone with water. The ride suddenly became great fun as balloons and props surprised and entertained us each time we went around.

It's as if the pirate was earning points to be the best ride in the park. He created added value, especially for us older folk. What do we do to create added value to people we meet every day. How will they remember us? What is unique about you?

23 April

There is no fooling some people. We were out for a meal as a family. The welcome we received was warm and friendly. The waiter was very attentive to the kids, which delighted them and us. The setting was beautiful, and the décor was tasteful and fun. Our drinks arrived promptly, and the waiter took great pride in helping us choose from an extensive a la carte menu. The main courses arrived with silver domes for presentation that were removed simultaneously for great effect. We said our thank-yous and began our meal.

We looked at each other in disappointment as Brian's stuffed chicken breast, wrapped in chorizo with freshly steamed vegetables, was dry and barely stuffed. The chorizo was plonked on top with peas and sweet corn mush. My cod dish was barely recognisable.

How was a restaurant like this still open for business? What a shame, as we were out for a family meal. The kids, however, learnt a valuable lesson; Things are not always as they seem. We also discussed the importance of always being genuine and authentic, and never disguise who you really are!

24 April

Love is patient and love is kind.
Love is precious and is easy to find.
Love believes and endures all things.
Love is what makes our hearts sing.
Love is strong and love is bold.
Love is happiness so keep a hold.
Love is nature and love is light.
Love is forever and ever, especially as we say 'goodnight.'

Vanessa Stottor

25 April

"Ladder of judgement." I heard this the other day and thought it was brilliant. After many years of being judged by my husband's choices, I have made every effort to be accepting of everyone all the time. When we stand on the ladder of judgement, there is someone above us and someone below us, so our view of others is not always correct.

If we climb down from the ladder of judgement and stand on the ground, on the same level as everyone else, our perspective is different, and we are more accepting of others. We want others to be more accepting of us, so I believe it's only fair we are of others first.

26 April

I now write everything down as a result of huge adversity. It really helped me clear my head and see things from a different perspective.

Dear Diary I tell you all my secrets, from deep within my mind
You never sit in judgement, you are silent and refined.
I talk to you every day, you are my closest friend
I can pour out my heart to you, on you I can depend.
My thoughts, actions and feelings—a record is always kept,
The times I've laughed or misbehaved, the many times I've wept.
So as I sit and write to you, I ponder, with a frown
How to express what I have to say, I need to get it down.
For some day in the future, I'll want to know, I'm sure
Of what I did back in the past and how I felt before.
So keep within your pages, my stories good and bad
Of things that made me happy and times when I was sad.
Tell no-one of your contents, what lies within your heart,
The ramblings of a lady who has too much to impart.
So save it all dear Diary, for one day when I'm old,
Your pages I will turn once more and my stories can be told.

Trudie Stottor

27 April

Write your own story. If you could forward your life twenty, thirty, or forty years, what would it look like if you could create it exactly how you want it to look? I often imagine my life and how I would like it to look. I even did so when I was a child at school, which is probably why my reports said, "Vanessa is constantly daydreaming out of the window."

Now I know it isn't a bad thing but necessary to visualise. If you could write to your ten-year-old self, what would you say? What would you focus on, and what would you change, if anything?

Are you living your life as you designed? Have some fun. Write to yourself about your life until now and then from this point on about the life you have designed.

Write your own story.

28 April

You *can* be the one to make a difference! In this big wide world, we think we are insignificant, but we are not. Imagine yourself as leaving a trail of magic dust behind you; you never know who is going to want to follow it. We *all* have something to offer, something that will make a difference, even to just one person. You might not always think what you have to offer is much, but it could be everything to another person. A small gesture—say, letting someone in front of you in a queue if they seem in a hurry—will create good feelings in the person and these feelings are passed on to someone else, and so on!

Making a difference to just one person makes all the difference to many others. *You* can be the one to make a difference.

29 April

A simple question that can make a huge difference every day: "What have you learnt today?" When you ask yourself this question, can you give yourself a good answer? Ask yourself this question every night before going to bed.

Wherever possible, I look for the lesson to be learnt in all situations. It has made me more open-minded and more tolerant of others. Whether it be small or life-changing, all lessons are valuable. I often talk situations through with the children and ask them what they have learnt. I believe it makes them more aware of the world around them.

How could your life or your children's lives be immeasurably enhanced by adding this question, or one like it, to your daily routine? In what way could you make this question as fundamental as eating or sleeping? What have you learnt today?

30 April

As a result of yesterday's message, this is what I learnt today. Always listen to children's valuable comments! My daughter and I were driving along, and I said, "What pretty houses."

Liberty, who is ten years old, said, "Just because they are pretty on the outside doesn't mean they are pretty on the inside."

Wow! How many of us judge a book by its cover? How many of us stick with our first impressions? Maybe today we can try and not judge a book by its cover and really make the effort to take the time to get to know the book inside.

Would you want someone to judge you by your cover or take time to get to know you?

1 May

Somebody once said to me, "You only get one chance at life. If you don't do it now, when are you going to do it?" We may have heard this many times, but I heard it at a time that gave me such clarity. If I wasn't going to do it now, when was I going to do it? If I didn't step up to the plate and be brave now, when else would I get the chance? Tomorrow? Tomorrow never comes! Whatever it is we need to do to grow our business, make a difference, or become a better person.

Step up to do it now, or when else will you get the chance? Do it now!

2 May

Do you worry every day? Has it become a habit? A wise man once said, "Why worry about something you have no control over, because if you have no control over it, there is no point in worrying. Why worry about something you do have control over, because if you do have control over it, then there is no point in worrying about it." This eliminates all there is to worry about. So simple, but so true! I'm sure we all know someone who constantly worries. To worry is to live in fear, and fear is a negative emotion. To feel negative is hard work and can attract more fear to you to worry about. Where possible, try to focus on what is good and healthy about your life. We all have so much to be grateful for.

3 May

Being the month of May, we should be woken by bright rays of sunshine through our bedroom windows. This is not always the case, so it is up to us to be the sunshine people want to see. Science says we are bundles of energy and that our energies radiate out. So be that friendly, warm, and happy person you are and the sunshine people want to see. When our energies are raised, by being happy and friendly, they become higher and faster, so you raise the energies of others by just being in their space. It's a fact!

Think how quickly good feelings can spread if we all become rays of sunshine for the next person. The more of your higher energy you give away, the more you are attracting back to you, making you a constant ray of sunshine to brighten anyone's day.

4 May

Be careful what you wish for, as you might just get it. Our subconscious minds are key. What we plant is what grows. A homeless man says, "All I want is £1 to buy some food and a drink." With his eyes fixed firmly on the ground, hoping someone has dropped a £1 coin, he shuffles up and down the street.

A woman tries in vain to attract his attention. "Sir," she calls. "Excuse me, sir." She smiles.

He looks up, sees she is also homeless, and thinks, *She can't help me*. He grunts and carries on down the street. He does find his £1 coin later in the day, but perhaps if he had asked for a warm shelter, with a square meal and enough to drink, he would have realised that was exactly what the homeless woman was offering. She was on her way back to the homeless shelter and wanted to take him with her. Instead, he got what he asked for, a £1 coin to buy a bread roll and some water. But no place to stay.

The greatest danger is not that our hopes are too high and we miss them. It is that they are too low and we do!

5 May

To remind yourself of the power of persistence, consider the metaphor of the stonecutter. How does he break open a giant boulder? He whacks it as hard as he can. The first hit doesn't leave even a scratch, but again he strikes, hundreds, maybe thousands of times.

The stonecutter persists even when his actions seem to be futile. But he knows that just because you don't see immediate results, it doesn't mean you're not making progress. So he keeps striking the rock. At some point it doesn't just chip but literally splits in two. Did the final blow break open the boulder? Of course not. It was the constant pressure being applied to the challenge at hand.

How can you apply this metaphor to your life in order to passionately persist? The end is so much more rewarding when you persist.

6 May

Affirmations: daily words that you repeat. When I wake up in the morning, I say to myself, "Thank you for this morning. I attract all great things to me, and I radiate love."

It is so important to have affirmations, as it trains the mind to think only what you feed it! Write your own affirmations to fit with your own goals, whether it be in business or to have your loved ones safe and well. It is also important to use positive words that refer to the present. For example, "I have all I dreamed of in my life right now. Thank you," or, "I am in perfect health. Thank you." Start with simple phrases and learn to build your affirmations. They will transform your life!

7 May

Would you like to be thought of as interesting? Traditional thinking says if we want to be considered interesting, you first have to be well read, bright, articulate, charming, and witty.

I believe this is not the case. There was a story of a man who tried and tested this theory. He sat between two people on a plane, asked them questions about themselves, and let them talk. He did this on seven plane journeys in one week. As he had their details, they were all later contacted. *All* said they didn't know where he lived or what he did for a living, but 70 percent said he was one of the most interesting people they ever met.

If you want to be thought of as an interesting person, be interested rather than interesting.

8 May

Are you attracted to different flowers. Do you know they all mean different things. My dear friend Sarah Devereux, from Portia Potts floristry (*www.portiapotts.com*), shared with me the meanings of some flowers. I was pleased to find my favourite flower, the orchid, means ecstasy, an overwhelming feeling of great happiness or joyful excitement. What is your favourite flower? Here are a few with their meanings.

- Red rose—love
- Carnation—health, energy, love
- Dahlia—dignity, elegance
- Daisy—innocence
- Freesia—calmness
- Heather—passion
- Hibiscus—opportunity
- Honeysuckle—bond of love
- Jasmine—good luck
- Pansy—thoughtfulness
- Poppy—dreams
- Primrose—hope
- Sunflower—power

Are you, like me, now going to see our beautiful world of flowers in a whole new light? Thank you, Sarah.

9 May

The power of influence! Who and what influence your decisions? Who do you surround yourself with every day? Can you write down the six people you spend most time with and say they empower you, make you feel alive, and encourage you? Who are your influences at work, home, and amongst your friends?

I surround myself daily with people who empower me, and I feel I can take on the world! So pick carefully the people in your circle of influence. Select those who truly care about you and your passions. In turn, you will be of influence to others.

10 May

Live by the 80/20 rule. You don't always have control as to what happens to you in your day (represented by 20 percent), but you can control how you react to it (represented by 80 percent).

I remember the story of a family having breakfast and the little girl spills coffee on her dad. Dad gets cross and starts shouting, little girls cries, dad stomps upstairs to change clothes, mum consoles little girl, dad's late for work, little girl misses school bus, everyone is upset. And their day goes from bad to worse. Or at breakfast the little girl spills the coffee on her dad, and he says, "Careful sweetie. Did it spill on you?" Mum mops up coffee, Dad swiftly changes clothes, everyone finishes breakfast, Dad drops little girl at school bus and leaves her with a hug and a kiss, Dad gets to work early, everyone is happy and content. All have a wonderful day because of how they chose to react to a coffee spillage.

We can choose how we react to what life gives us. Decide to live by the 80/20 rule.

11 May

Act as if. If we live each day as if we already are who we would like to be, is it possible that would boost our self-confidence and our self-belief? We all know the importance of having a visual goal, a five-year plan, and a dream we wish to aspire to. Is there a different you not brave enough to come out? Then act as if! When you don't know how to do something, flip it, and act as if you do. If you behave as if you already are who you want to be, you will be amazed about how you behave and how others behave towards to you!

We all have to start somewhere. If we act as if, we are more likely to look more confident, and this will give us the edge we need to act as if.

Something to think about!

12 May

How many of us have learnt to say, "Next"? Maybe you play tennis or squash, and you have a run of bad shots. Because the brain is focused on the last bad shot, you play another and so on. Or maybe a similar situation happens at work or with friends, and you say the same thing because of habit. Train yourself to say, "Next." The brain doesn't differentiate between what's real and what's strongly imagined. Create your own phrase.

- Poor telephone conversation—Next call!
- Not sure what to say when meeting someone—Next words!
- Not getting something done—Next action!
- Your suggestion gets rejected—Next idea!

The answers you need are all within you!

13 May

How do you want to be remembered?

When you leave a room, a conversation, a situation, what impression have you left?

In a crowded place, whatever you like, people always remember a happy, smiling face. It's infectious! Be the person who made others feel better about themselves when you were with them!

14 May

Cherish what you have! Thieves can take your possessions, but they cannot take what truly belongs to you: your heart, your mind, and what you believe.

Whom do I love? What do I think? What do I believe?

Cherish what truly is yours!

15 May

If you want to have more, you have to *be* more! There is the universal Golden Rule: "Do unto others as you would have them do unto you." Do we always go the extra mile for someone else? Do we hold doors open for others? Do we give someone 50p for the car park he or she has no change? Do we help others carry their shopping to their cars? Do we pay others genuine compliments?

For one day, make it your purpose to be all about the other person, and last thing at night, see how great you feel.

Today is the day it is all about the other person.

Today is the day I will be more, and I will be of service to others!

16 May

Love and learn! Make the most out of every day; you never know what is around the corner. Learn to see the good in every situation. However much of a challenge we may find this in difficult or bad situations, it is a real gift to do and such a huge lesson to learn.

Learn how to send love to every difficult situation. Again, however hard we may find this, we gain a sense of peace from sending love at time of difficulty.

Appreciate every day and every situation. Love and learn!

17 May

Don't you just love sunny days? Sunny days, for me, are such a blessing, and I feel like I could skip everywhere! When it is sunny, we find ourselves so much more aware of everything around us. We take off our blinkers and notice more of the beauty that is all around us. We tend to feel more open-minded and willing to do more. It's easy to love a sunny day, and it's easy to love the cheerful moods of others on a sunny day. We love to be out doing what we love on a sunny day!

Doing what you love is the cornerstone of having abundance in your life!

18 May

A child's wise words. When my little girl, Liberty, was nearly three years old, she came home from preschool with a picture she had drawn of herself. It was a typical child's drawing: circle for her head with two dots for eyes, a dot for her nose, and a big cheesy smile; a triangle for her body, with stick arms, fingers, legs, and toes. The wonderful thing about her drawing was the circle above her head which she called her hat. It resembled a halo. We were all intrigued by her hat.

A day or so later, we were having dinner, and my dad said to me, "Ask her who she is."

Now bearing in mind Liberty was nearly three, her response floored us all. "Me?" she asked. "Don't you know? I'm the one who put the arrows on this planet for you to follow," she said very matter-of-factly as she got up from the table and walked out of the room. We were all dumbfounded, as I'm not sure expected that response.

I truly believe Liberty is a very special little girl, which is why I call her "my angel" and always will. Why is it that children say such wonderful things, and we do not always pay attention? From that day forward, I have been fascinated by any child's wise words!

19 May

Each of us is a limited edition, special and unique in our ways. We brighten the universe for a planetary moment, enlightening the world with rare and precious gifts. Wrapped in brilliance—a splash of magnificent glory released in slow motion. We are passion lit from within, a living journey seeking and giving light.

Cheryl Gholar

We are made of energy. Do you put all that energy to good use? If you don't think of yourself as unique, why not? If you do think of yourself as unique, good! Why? Start by feeling grateful: feeling gratitude and not expressing it is like wrapping a present and not giving it. How silly!

"We brighten the universe for a planetary moment."

20 May

I woke up thinking,

- Are you understood?
- Do you speak clearly?
- Do you say what you really mean?
- Do you hear only what you want to hear?
- Do you take time to listen and hear more than just words?
- Do you listen with your heart?

21 May

Are you driving your life into the future looking in the rear-view mirror to guide yourself? If you are, you'll crash. Are you making the same mistakes over and over again, rather than having the courage to do something new until it works? "It's no use, I've tried everything. That's it!" You haven't tried everything, or you'd have found something works. How many of us have personal power and courage to do something different until it works. Not many! And that is why we keep making the same mistakes.

Tap into your personal power, and Be Bold, Be Beautiful and Be Brilliant!

22 May

There's never a failure, just a lesson! Turn a failure into a triumph.

The story of the post-it was a failure turned into a triumph. 'Mr Post-it' was trying to invent a glue that never came unstuck. As we know today, the Post-it is a piece of paper that can be stuck and restuck! Genius! As a result of originally "failing" to produce a glue that never came unstuck, the result was a multimillion-pound product that is now worldwide! I think it is safe to say that this failure was a triumph.

There is always a lesson to be learnt, and that is the success! So next time you feel despondent, sit back and find the lesson to be learnt.

23 May

To get new results, we have to take new action. How?

Decision: The power of decision is the power of change.

We don't always have control over what happens to us, but we do have control over how we decide to react. All answers are within us! How do you deal with a problem? How do you decide to deal with it?

It is in your moments of decision that your destiny is shaped.

Back up your decision with action. There must be action for your decision to materialise.

24 May

Do you think of yourself as a candle, a beautiful, fragrant candle? What does it take to ignite your candle and release your fragrance so others can see the way and follow your greatness?

- You are an everlasting candle.
- Light is a powerful, positive energy that will brighten any dark corner.
- Use positive thoughts and actions to reignite your light when blown out.
- Always remember darkness fades when light arrives.

25 May

Ever been tempted to give up on a goal or an ambition because it just seemed unattainable? Well, imagine you are a clock. A clock has to tick over thirty million times each year, a huge number. But, of course, the clock doesn't have to worry about the enormity of its task, because it gets there one tick at a time. Now take another look at that impossible goal, and ask yourself how far you might get if you just go one tick at a time.

We clearly worry ourselves with how big our goals and ambitions seem. When if we just concentrate on each possible step and stay focused, give me one reason why the impossible cannot be done?

Impossible is just a question of spacing. I'm possible!

26 May

Two teachers worked in classrooms side by side for many years. They were also longstanding friends, but it was widely known their teaching styles were very different. One was renowned for loudness of her voice, and, indeed, she could often be heard in the other classrooms.

In the infant class next door, however, Elaine's voice was never heard outside the room, and her pupils were always as quiet as proverbial mice. Someone asked her what her secret was. "It happened by accident," she explained. "Once when I had just started teaching, I almost lost my voice. I could only whisper, yet I discovered that the softer I spoke, the quieter the children became, and the more closely they listened! I adopted that approach, and it has held me in good stead for almost forty years."

Never underestimate the power of a whisper. In this noisy world, how good it is to know you don't have to be loud to gain attention!

27 May

How big is your belief system? What is your heart's desire? Do you know it's OK to dream big? Many people have dreams but no belief system to back them up.

What is a belief system? Belief is what's in your heart, and what makes it strong or worthy of believing in are your experiences. Everyone has experiences, and the great news is your brain remembers everything, and your body knows everything! So ask your brain to remember good things about yourself and what you've done. Ask yourself questions, as we all have the answers within. All experiences strengthen your belief system.

28 May

Motivation

Motive	Action
Purpose	Movement
Reason	To a
Why	Goal

Motivated people are successful. Successful people are motivated. So know your reason why. Have a goal and act on it, and you will have the motivation to succeed.

29 May

Pay attention! What you see is what you get.

Focus on good stuff ⟶ good stuff
Focus on bad stuff ⟶ bad stuff

A car skidding out of control—don't focus on lamp post, or you'll hit it. Focus in other directions, and you're more likely to be guided in another direction.

When we change our focus or try something new, it can take a while for the ship to change direction. Stay focused, and your ship will turn soon enough.

30 May

Where do you want to be one year from now? Do you have a dream? Do you dare to dream a dream.

Susan Boyle was just an ordinary woman and is now a worldwide star, because she believed she was "meant to be."

It is possible, if you just allow yourself to dream.

31 May

The questions are the answers. It's all about asking the *right* questions.

Make sure you ask yourself the right questions. A great place to start is, "What am I happy about today? Who loves me, and whom do I love? What makes me feel happy and content?"

The answers come rolling in when you ask the right questions. Be inquisitive, and listen to the answers you get.

1 June

I am often asked, "Why are you always so happy?" I do think it strange sometimes when people ask me that, but then I think, *Maybe they haven't learnt the art of gratitude!*

"I can move my legs, shake my arms, and see you! I have air in my lungs and a sound mind," are what most people can say. Do we take for granted the most obvious things? Is gratitude the one thing we're missing?

Remind yourself of what you have now. What if one day we woke up and all we had was what was important to us, and all our worries and problems disappeared. Would we be happy?

Be grateful for what is in your life now, and it will make the world of difference.

2 June

True colours. Do you know your true colours? Do you know what makes you, you?

Know your true colours. Let them shine through. Don't be afraid to let them shine through; they are beautiful, like a rainbow!

How colourful is your rainbow? Would it brighten someone else's day? Our true colours are why people love us.

Know your true colours and let them shine through.

3 June

How many of us are calm or silent for a period of time in our day? We all lead such busy lives that we don't have time to be still. We have sixty thousand thoughts a day. That's a lot of chatter. We know thoughts are energy, so by being still, calm, and quiet for a few moments a day, we can reduce our thoughts to twenty thousand.

Liken your mind to a pond. On the surface it collects all the rubbish and, at times, can look dirty. It has movement. Underneath there is not so much rubbish, and there is less movement. Deeper down, it is really calm and serene, less noisy!

If we take time for silence, our minds can be less noisy and busy. Silence is what makes the music; otherwise, it would just be one long noise! Would you rather listen to a load of busy noise or beautiful music? Enjoy your silent moments.

4 June

Mimic confident people. Change the pattern of the way you move, gesture, and speak. Send a message through your nervous system back to your brain about what you expect from yourself. It will change your feelings and mindset. You'll have more powerful, positive thoughts and actions. Do it obviously and with intention in the beginning, and it will become a positive, powerful habit within your mind and nervous system. Copy what confident, successful people do. The way they walk, talk, and their body language. You'll positively start influencing those around you. Fake it until you make it!

5 June

We can have all the qualifications in the world, but it is experience that is the best teacher. Our experiences are valuable not only to us but also to others. All we experience is either good or bad and we have feelings attached to each experience. I believe this is what makes our experiences worth sharing. This, then, is the teacher for ourselves as well as for others. Let your experiences be the teacher.

6 June

Living in the past? Let go of your personal history. Imagine you're driving a speedboat. When you look behind, what do you see? A wake. That is your past, your personal history. Is *it* driving the boat? No, *you* are. It's behind you, and there's nothing you can do about it.

We often look at our past to remind us of what we can't do or what's hurt us. What if you wake up with amnesia? Would it change how you behave today? If we say we've never failed just learnt lessons, what would you do with the lessons learnt?

Live for today, not yesterday. Learn from the past; it's all you can do. Leave the wake behind you, and drive the boat to where you want to go.

7 June

Ever feel you are backed into a corner, stuck in a hole? Not knowing how to climb out or break through the wall? Try adjusting your vocabulary. Words drastically change how we feel, think, and view the world.

Feeling overwhelmed? Try saying, "I'm in demand." Feeling irritated? You're stimulated. Rejected? No, misunderstood. Feeling lost? You're searching.

It works the other way, too. Feel fine? You feel phenomenal. Awake? You're energised. Fortunate? You are unbelievably blessed.

Surely it's worth a try for a week or three, until it becomes a habit. Then look back, and notice the difference.

I feel energised and unbelievably blessed to be living in a beautiful world.

How do you feel today?

8 June

All the answers we need are within us. Dig down deep to learn how to solve a problem. When you feel inspired, you feel like you can do anything! Go to a quiet place, dig down deep, and get inspiration from anywhere you feel right. You'll be surprised what you find. Think of it this way, do you think moving the clouds makes the sun shine? No, the sun is always there; the clouds just hide it.

What is your sun, and what is hiding it? It's there, and we know it is. Let's remove the clouds and shine bright on all our cares and concerns.

9 June

There's always going to be another mountain, I'm always going to want to make it move, always an uphill battle, sometimes I'm going to have to lose, it's not about how fast I get there, it's not about what's waiting on the other side, it's the climb!

Miley Cyrus

These lyrics remind us we must keep our eyes open and enjoy the ride of life.

Enjoy your ride today.

10 June

Here's a puzzle for you! Can you guess the answer?

It's something that makes you happy in the house, spells goodwill in business, takes up just a moment of time, and stops anybody from being sad. It's like sunshine when you're down. it costs nothing to buy, no electricity to operate and makes you happy when repeated. Yes, that's right. It's a smile!"

Don't you agree that we should all be more aware of the simplest things in life?

11 June

I wish you enough sun to keep your attitude bright.

I wish you enough rain to appreciate the sun more.

I wish you enough happiness to keep your spirit alive.

I wish you enough pain so that the smallest joys in life appear much bigger.

I wish you enough gain to satisfy your wanting.

I wish you enough loss to appreciate all that you possess.

I wish enough "Hello's" to get you through the final "Goodbye."

Anon

What I took from these words was we only have happen to us what our Higher Power knows we can handle to make us stronger. it also made me rethink about how grateful I am!

Be grateful every day for every small thing. I wish enough of all you need today, especially enough love to give away for it to come back tenfold to you.

12 June

I have salt and pepper pots filled with imaginary dust. I shake them over me when needed. Try it. Amazing things happen. How about filling the pots with happiness dust or courage dust. There are times when we all need something to help us along the way. We all have it, but we don't always use it to its full advantage. Yes, our minds.

13 June

There are 206 named bones in the adult human body. All very scientific and interesting, however I prefer this.

> You only need three bones to journey successfully through life, a wishbone to dream with, a backbone for the courage to get through the hard times and a funny bone to laugh at life along the way!

I found this painted onto a canvas at a craft fair and loved it.

Don't you find we complicate things too much? We need to remind ourselves often to keep it simple. Dream, be courageous, and laugh along the way.

14 June

You live in your own little insignificant corner of a small planet. How important can you make yourself? Well, try looking at it all from a different point of view. "If Earth is that small, how small am I? Just a speck in the universe. But yet significant enough that God would create me, love me, and touch my life." That's how important you are!

Sometimes we feel insignificant and unimportant. Yet to some people, we are their world. God didn't have time to make a nobody, only a somebody! And that somebody is you!

So even though we may be a speck in the universe, so is everyone else. Why do we notice some people but not others? Because they've decided not to be insignificant. They've decided to feel important. We can all do that! You are important!

15 June

Are you still learning? Life's teachers are not always who you expect. When you are ready to learn, teachers make themselves present. You need to keep your eyes open. There's a story of the little girl who went to a friend's for tea. The mum was obese. At the door, the little girl said to her friend, "I didn't know your mummy was fat!" Right there and then was the lesson/teacher that woman needed to lose her weight.

We'd also like to think the little girl learnt her lesson—to always be polite and her parents to about how to be tactful.

As we get older, we may think we no longer need to learn. That's where the problem lies. If you stop learning, you stop living. So when you're truly ready, the teachers will make themselves present. It's the law of the universe!

16 June

Your life is a play! Have you ever thought of it that way? Everyone has a part to play. Some people only perform in the first act, some play a bigger part, some are extras, and so on.

Ultimately, you are the director and play the lead role! So you have control over how the story is played. You will have villains; they make a play interesting, don't they? And there is always a hero.

But what keeps you on the edge of your seat is that the story is interesting and exciting. If the storyline is flat, you will fall asleep. So remember that your play is interesting; there are ups and downs. It's exciting when people win, and it's sad when people get hurt. A great storyline will keep you on your toes.

Fill your play with key people and lots of interest, and you can have the production you've always wanted. Lights, camera, action!

17 June

Don't we often use "tomorrow" as the time we'll start something?

Tomorrow never comes. We need to remind ourselves of the good around us. It's like the song lyrics for the song titled 'Feeling Good'. "It's a new dawn, it's a new day, it's a new life, for me, and I'm feeling good!"

Treat each day as a new beginning. It's worth a try. Live for today, a new day, a new beginning! Life is a celebration of awakenings, beginnings, and wonderful surprises that awaken the soul. Tomorrow never comes. Today is the time to be present

18 June

The relay race could be a way to explain how we view passing on knowledge. It's in the way things we know or learn are passed to the next generation and the next. When one of us discovers a new insight into something, comes up with a scientific discovery, or finds something that improves the lot of ordinary people, the benefit gets handed on. The new generation builds on the knowledge and passes it on to the next.

It's rather nice to think of human wisdom being passed on, like a baton. If we can each play our own small part, it's one race we all can win!

19 June

As to story goes, a man saw a scorpion struggling in a deep pool of water. He decided to try to save it by stretching out a finger, but the creature instantly stung him. Again, the man tried to remove the scorpion from the water, but he was stung again. An onlooker urged him to give up and go home. But the would-be rescuer said, "It is the nature of the scorpion to sting. It is my nature to love. Why should I give up my nature because it is contrary to the way of the scorpion?"

That's a classic! How many of us stop the way we are, because it is different than someone else's? From now on, have convictions in your actions, and believe in who you are. It's what makes you, you. Too many people behave a certain way so they fit in. Be your own person, and enjoy who you are!

20 June

Peaceful place. Do you have a peaceful place to go when it all gets overwhelming? This place is somewhere safe and beautiful. There is no one there but you. It's quiet and calming, and you base yourself there just for a while. Only you know about it, and you can get there in an instant.

Create this special place for you, and leave your troubles behind. This place is yours; create it in your mind.

21 June

Australia's Great Barrier Reef resembles life brilliantly. The landward, sheltered side is murky and dull, while the seaward side is vibrant and full of life. It's the seaward side that struggles every day because of ocean currents, tides, and storms. As a result, that side of the reef becomes stronger, brighter, more alive.

So the next time you feel challenged, just think of the Great Barrier Reef. It's a natural wonder of the world, and so are you! I think it's worth remembering the powers that be give us only what we can handle to make us stronger and a better person. When we think about it that way, we should feel quite flattered we're able to deal with all we do. You're a natural wonder of the world!

22 June

Guardian angels come in all shapes and sizes. You might be living with one. Keep a lookout today! When I find a small white feather on the ground, it makes me smile. I pretend an angel has left it there for me to find as a sign I am looked after.

We are guided daily by those in our lives and by what we can't see. Be an angel for someone else.

23 June

It's a glorious, sunny day, but we can still feel weary. Are you running on empty? Want to give more than you have at the moment? Liken yourself to a coffee pot. Fill yourself with love and energy. Then you have enough to pour onto others.

Sit somewhere still and quiet. Close your eyes. You are a coffee pot. Take off your lid and ask to be filled with love, energy, and whatever else you feel you need in your life at that moment. Replace your lid. Say, "Thank you." Now you have enough to go and pour onto others. I do this often and find the analogy of the coffee pot easy to visualise.

24 June

The fisherman catches a crab, puts it in the wicker basket, and puts the lid back on the basket. He catches a second crab and puts it in the basket, but he doesn't put the lid back on. Then he catches the third crab, puts it in the basket, and again doesn't put the lid back on the basket. As the third crab tries to crawl out of the basket, the other crabs claw it back in. So the crab remains in the basket.

Don't let negative, crabby people hold you back. Instead, surround yourself with positive, loving people who inspire you. You can climb out of the basket!

25 June

What if the "hokey cokey" *is* what it's all about? Knees bend, arms stretch, ra, ra, ra!

Do we take life too seriously? When we're relaxing and enjoying our families, friends, and work, doesn't everything all slip into place? So next time it all seems a bit overwhelming, I'm definitely going to visualise myself doing the hokey cokey. And maybe if no one's watching, actually *do* the hokey cokey, and shake it all about. That is more than likely going to put a smile on my face. You know what they say, dance like nobody's watching! Maybe so we don't look too daft, we could involve the kids. It's definitely worth a try!

26 June

Do we fully appreciate that our faces can give the game away? Our faces say so much, as does our body language. People tend to treat us the way we say we want to be treated. If we walk about with a frown on our face and our arms crossed, we are not going to get too many people smiling and saying, "Hello."

What message are you giving on your face and in your body language? It really makes a difference in how people treat you!

Have an expressive day!

27 June

Albert Einstein said, "There are only two ways to live your life. One is as though nothing is a miracle. The other is as though everything is a miracle." From the moment we get up in the morning until we close our eyes at night, we are witnesses to miracles. Sprinkled throughout each day, we'll find them, if we take time to look, in a sunrise, birds singing, an encouraging word spoken at just the right time, or perhaps a piece of music that inspires. Wherever you go, keep an eye open for miracles. Miracles make life colourful and are all around us, waiting to be noticed!

Sometimes we think miracles are big things that happen. But it isn't the case. Expect miracles to happen, and they will. Miracles surround us daily, so wherever you go, keep an eye open for miracles.

28 June

Daily Survival Kit

Toothpick—to remind you to pick out the best qualities in others

Rubber Band—to remind you to be flexible

Pen—to remind you to list your blessings every day

Tube of Glue—to remind you to stick with it; you can accomplish that task

Teabag—to remind you to relax daily

Bandage and Plasters—to remind you to heal hurt feelings, yours and someone else's

Life is really quite simple, but we do a great job of complicating it. It's a lot easier to appreciate life when the sun is shining and showing the natural world at its best.

The world turns with such little effort. Maybe we should, too.

29 June

There once was a story of a farmer who couldn't afford to keep his donkey. So he hid it in a well and covered it with sand to hide the evidence. What the farmer didn't realise was that every time the shovel of sand landed on the donkey's back, the donkey shook it off. Over time, the sand began to layer under the donkey, and soon enough, the donkey used it to climb out of the well. Amazing!

I love this story. The moral of this story is when life throws stuff at you that knocks you off your perch, use it to your advantage. Find the opportunity in all that comes your way, good and bad. Turn obstacles into stepping stones, and free yourself.

30 June

Break the habit! Did you know it takes twenty-one days to break or create a habit? A habit is something we do over and over again. It can be a good or a bad habit.

Let's create a new habit. A great place to start is with how we think. Start today. The best time is in the mornings; when you wake up; try a little earlier than normal. Have a few words to yourself, like, "Today I feel alive, today is going to be a great day!" Say them with meaning, conviction, and a smile. You can make up your own to be more specific to you! If nothing else, it gets you on the right track. The spoken word, with a smile, feelings, and emotion attached to it, will penetrate the mind and reach the heart, because this is how the subconscious mind communicates.

1 July

The other day I shared the story about a donkey stuck in the well. He shook off the sand being thrown on it, and eventually used the sand to climb out of the well. Do you think this man had the same philosophy?

Walt Disney died before Disney World was opened to the public, and his widow was asked to take part in the special ceremony to mark the occasion. When an official said to her, "I wish Walt could have seen this," Mrs Disney replied, "He did."

Vision is the ability to see and believe in the intangible. It's hope fulfilled because of fate and perseverance. Have the vision and the ability to turn life's obstacles into stepping stones, and you, too, can create your own Disney World. Why not?

2 July

"If the world was my classroom then life is my curriculum." I saw this on a girl's T-shirt the other day, and it made me think, *How different would we be as adults if that was our education?* Don't get me wrong, I think school is a must. I went to a beautiful school and had a wonderful time. But do we underestimate what our children learn from the outside world? Do we teach them to appreciate nature as a marvellous creation? What can they can learn from how other people behave and what other people say? Do they know their lives are made up of choices, and there are consequences for their actions? Cultures, foods, and religions from all around the world. Life is full of amazing wonders, and we all have the choice to experience.

If we take time to teach the children around us what life has to offer, I'm sure we, too, would learn more. Make your world the classroom.

3 July

What a great delight is a day of sunshine. A clear blue sky when the storm is over.

Those are the first two lines of that timeless Italian song "O Sole Mio," translated into English, of course. The storm is what makes the clear blue sky which follows so enjoyable. That might just be the reason for storms, to help us appreciate the good times, in the same way as trials and tribulations of life are sent to prepare us for the "great delight" to come. Surely the storms and the sunshine in our lives are what make it interesting! The happiest people don't necessarily have the best of everything. They just make the most of everything that comes their way.

4 July

Do whatever makes you happy! The kids' school reports arrived home, and a friend of mine said her little one's comments were OK. There was nothing outstanding about his work, and he had average marks. Maybe she thought he might have excelled in something!

She looked up from reading his report, and to her amazement he had built, from scratch, their family barbecue. He followed the instructions and put it together piece by piece. He is seven!

She knew he was going to be great! She is going to encourage him to do exactly what he wants to do. She said to me, "As long as he is happy, he will excel at his work as an adult, and he will be outstanding! That's all we can ask for."

Do whatever makes you happy, and you will excel!

5 July

'Perseverance' and 'determination.' Two of my favourite words. Not everyone has perseverance and determination, but they are necessary if we want to better ourselves. Think of children. Aren't they determined? When they want that biscuit before teatime, they don't give up asking. And they persevere until we give in or tea's on the table. How about athletes? All winning athletes persevere and are determined, and they probably have been for months while in training.

In our daily lives, we are required to persevere and to stay determined. One of my favourite sayings is, "Keep on keeping on!" After a while, it becomes easier and part of your character. So next time you feel like chucking in the towel, hold on for just a little longer, and you'll be amazed how much stronger you become.

6 July

Ask, believe, receive! This is a proven formula, a universal law! How many of us have used this formula and been amazed by the results. Maybe it's worked for you, but you don't even know it. Have you ever thought of something or someone and then it, or the person, has appeared? That is how it works!

I'm sure we all agree there is something out there, turning our world and making our grass grow. This same something answers our requests. All we need to do is ask for an experience, a person, a book, or whatever it is you need. Believe, really believe it's already there, and you shall receive. Easy! Well, the hard part is believing it is already there. There has to be unwavering belief, even when you can't see how it's going to manifest. Believing is the crucial part of the equation.

Ask, *believe,* receive!

7 July

How to deal with change. I suppose there are two ways to deal with change: accept it or not. Change is not always something that we warm to, as it can upset our routine and what we are familiar with. However, if we are looking for change in our lives, for whatever reason, we welcome it, because it does change our routine and what we are familiar with.

When change is unexpected, I think it's important to remember things happen for a reason, even if we may not know the reason immediately. If we believe what is happening is for the better eventually, we can take comfort in the fact we will benefit in the long run.

I'm sure we can all remember a time when change felt uncomfortable, but looking back now, you can see why it happened. Learn to embrace change as part of the process and part of your life's journey for the better.

8 July

Imagine being deaf, dumb, and blind. Helen Keller was born with all of these difficulties. But as an adult, she toured America, raising funds for the American Foundation for the Blind and campaigning for people with disabilities like hers, who were often housed in asylums. This inspirational woman came into this life with seemingly insurmountable problems, but she left it having discovered a great secret. "Life is an exciting business," she said, "And it is most exciting when it is lived for others."

I think we sometimes forget there are others in our life. We can become so obsessed with what we are doing that we can run off track. Having a purpose and living our daily lives with and for others is surely what it's all about. Life is most exciting when it is lived with and for others.

9 July

"I lived on top of one hill and the school was at the top of another hill. Nobody ever went to school by car—we didn't have any cars." You might be tempted to feel rather sorry for this schoolboy and his daily slog, but that little lad was Roger Bannister. "To and from school was training in itself," he admitted after becoming the first man to run a four-minute mile.

Difficulties can often help us achieve great things when seen from a later perspective. From this story, it's clear to see our lives are already mapped out for us, and I think the sooner we learn to go with it, the happier we will be. So all the hills we are climbing are preparing us for something later in life. Happy climbing!

10 July

The eagle, it seems, has a unique ability to conserve energy. It can lock its wings in the outstretched position, gliding instead of flapping, waiting for the next current of air to lift it higher. Our equivalent of that locking mechanism must surely be faith. The next time you feel yourself getting into a bit of a flap, stop and glide awhile, knowing that a wind of inspiration will be along shortly. Those who master this get fresh strength. They spread their wings and soar like eagles.

We all know this, but it's comfortable getting in a flap. We know what that feels like, and it's risky to glide, waiting for that wind of inspiration, I'm sure we've all thought, *Yes, but what if the wind never comes and I fall?* We have to trust and have faith in what we believe will carry us to greater heights.

Have an amazing day, and soar like an eagle.

11 July

A strong woman isn't afraid of anything, but a woman of strength shows courage in the midst of fear. A strong woman tries to avoid repeating the same mistakes, but a woman of strength realises life's mistakes can be blessings. A strong woman will walk with confidence, but a woman of strength knows she will be caught. A strong woman believes she is able to make the journey. A woman of strength believes the journey will make her able. The most important thing in life is knowing who you are and to be true to yourself.

12 July

It isn't the mountain ahead that wears you out, it's the grain of sand in your shoe. We sometimes concentrate or worry so much about the mountain ahead of us, we create hurdles for ourselves that keep tripping us up. Focus on today, what is happening now. This is what needs our attention. It keeps us on track, and when we glance back, we find ourselves further up the mountain than we thought.

There is only so much we can do; the rest is out of our hands. Someone once said to me, "I have a list every morning of what I have to do and a list for the universe to do for me." I love this idea. It's almost like having two of you. We really would get stuff done, wouldn't we? We wouldn't deliberately create obstacles to get in our way. So the more we focus on the job in hand for today, the easier our climb will be.

13 July

Think about your very best friend or someone you love dearly, a child, partner, or a parent. Think about how much fun you have with the person, how he or she makes you laugh, the conversations you have. Think about how if this person needed you, you'd be there and how you would do anything in your power to protect the person from any harm. You so enjoy being around the individual, just thinking about him or her makes you smile. Think how lucky you are to have someone like this in your life.

Can you see the person's face? Now imagine *your* face there! Your very best friend should be you! Before anyone else is kind to you, be kind to yourself. Before someone makes you laugh, learn to laugh at yourself. Learn to treat yourself well. Be your own very best friend.

14 July

The definition of a successful person is simply an ordinary person with extraordinary determination. You cannot keep a determined person from success. If you place stumbling blocks in their way, they will take them for stepping stones and will use them to climb to new heights. The one who succeeds has a goal, a dream, and makes their plans and follows them.

Mary Kay Ash

Think about it for a while. An ordinary person, well that's you and I. With extraordinary determination, this is where the numbers diminish. Why is it we lack determination? There could be many reasons. Turning stumbling blocks into stepping stones, clever, but again few of us do it. Simplify it; they who succeed have a goal, a dream, a plan, and gets going! Have an extraordinary day!

15 July

How we interpret things. My seven-year-old asked me for some "spring juice." I smiled at him and asked what that was. It suddenly dawned on me that it was summer fruit squash. Love him! He had his own interpretation. He knew what he meant and believed he was right in asking for spring juice.

We all think in different ways. Just because someone interprets things in a different way from us doesn't mean he or she is wrong. It made me smile! How we interpret things is key to how we think.

16 July

I saw an advert that said, "There is a reason why bald men don't buy a comb." Have a quick think about it. Do you spend time, effort, and/or money on things you don't need to? We all do!

The key has to be limiting our time and effort spent on penny jobs. It isn't satisfying, and it is not progression. We need to learn how to say no. Are you a compulsive helper? When asked to do something, you can't say no? Be really clear about how you spend your time, effort, and money. Remember, when there is something that really needs to be done, it's done! If you see something you really want, you find the money.

Always remember there is a reason bald men don't buy combs. Spend your time, effort, and money where it's needed.

17 July

There is only so much we can do. Do what you can, and let the strength of the universe do the rest. Our bodies are built for physical strength, while our minds are able to do so much more than we can even conceive. There is an easier way to get things done; let the universe do it. Do what you can, and do it to the best of your ability. Believe and trust the rest will be taken care of.

18 July

Yesterday, I had a very liberating experience. I tried on every single piece of clothing I have. I got fed up with having so many clothes and nothing to wear. How many of us open our wardrobe doors and stare at clothes, not knowing what fits, what's hidden behind other clothes, what's suitable for today, and so on? I am now left with a wardrobe of clothes and can now see each item. The best bit is it's like I've been shopping, as I now have lots of "new" clothes (ones I forgot I had).

Why not do the same with our heads? Clear all the unnecessary chatter and damaging thoughts, and have a sort out. Replace negative thoughts with positive, happy, and loving ones. Each time you open the doors to your mind, you'll be met by only positive thoughts! How lovely!

Have a wonderful day!

19 July

Have you ever sat and watched people go about their day? In the park, on a beach, on the trains, people are amazing! How do they interact with others? Do they smile? I learn such a lot by watching others. I look for body language; how do they hold themselves? If they are engaging with someone else, are they interested? Are their arms open, letting others in, or are they crossed, shutting others out. Do they smile? It's amazing how many people don't smile, and if you smile at them, they think you're weird. Then there are people who we learn from; they're smiling, their arms are open and welcoming, and their bodies are relaxed. They don't even have to say very much, because their body language says it all. "I am confident, happy, relaxed."

Make sure you are giving the right impression with how your body moves. Make a difference today!

20 July

Do you have a role model? Have you ever heard the saying, "Hitch your wagon to a star"?

It's so important to have a role model. This might be someone you admire, someone familiar, a special friend or family member, or you could have a few. It has to be someone who is walking the walk and talking the talk, someone who aspires to become a better person, someone who practices the Golden Rule, and someone going in the same direction as you—forward! Pick wisely, as one day this role model could be you!

Hitch your wagon to their star. Your perfect role model will be glad to show you the way!

21 July

I heard a fabulous saying from a great colleague. "I know you think you understand what I said, but I'm not sure you understood what I mean." Brilliant! Don't you think half our problem is that people misunderstand what we mean? Are we choosing the wrong words? Are we speaking just words with no tone or expression? Words can be so hurtful if said in the wrong way, equally if they are misunderstood by the person listening. This is why it is so important to choose your words carefully. Try to be as clear and expressive as you can. If you can create a picture with your words, you may be more easily understood.

A classic sentence for not just hearing words but understanding them: "It's not what you think you are but what you think you are!"

22 July

Jodi left his infant school yesterday, and the teachers gave him a memory book of photos and best bits of his work since he joined the school. Got me thinking, *What would my book of memories look like?* If we could create a book of memories, what would you put in yours? Photos of your loved ones, records of achievements? A record of special occasions, birthdays, holidays, pictures of places and scenery around the world? All your favourite things?

Live your life and do what you would like to do as if it were going into a book of memories. Would you think and do things differently if you knew it was going in a book? Have fun creating an imaginary book of memories of your own.

23 July

Aren't Disney films amazing? Every time I watch one, it teaches me so much. Yesterday, I saw *Toy Story 3* with the children. The main story was about a group of toys that had been special to a boy called Andy. Andy was now grown up and going to college. So he was sorting out what was for the attic and what was for the bin. The toys, all bar Woody, Andy's favourite, were mistakenly donated to a children's nursery.

To cut a long story short, they were being tormented by the other toys, so they tried to escape to be with Woody. It was an amazing story that brought a tear to my eye, as they all stayed together because they worked best together. Whether in a team in business or with friends or family, always work together to get the impossible done!

24 July

Wouldn't it be nice if someone said told you there is no such thing as a mistake? What if this were true? How about, "There are no mistakes when making a conviction."

When you have a belief that is the path, there are no mistakes. So if you're going from A to B, as you believe to be the right path, and take a wrong turn, use it as a rest stop to fill up your tank, freshen up, and have a bite to eat. Then you're ready to get back on the right track. Some may look at it as a mistake. But if you get back on the right track, there was no mistake, only a chance to recharge.

Look at so-called mistakes growth or learning curves. You would almost welcome these mistakes if you knew they would make you stronger.

25 July

How to look good naked! Don't worry, I'm not going to ask you to strip and start prancing down the high street. Use your imagination! What I want you to do is take off all your jewellery. Put your phone, iPod, laptop, and handbag on the table. Imagine yourself not having house and all your possessions. Stand in front of a mirror, wearing only your clothes of choice. All you should see in front of you is someone wearing a big smile. Everything that makes you look and feel great have been taken away.

Are you completely happy with your smile, your mind, and your heart? This is looking good naked! Your heart is big and warm, your mind is filled with only what you choose, and you have a big smile. Being completely comfortable with what you have to offer is the most important thing; accessories are a bonus. Do you look good naked?

26 July

Have you ever sat and watched someone show off his or her body? Yesterday we watched my husband in his first bodybuilding competition. These men and women were so passionate. Their bodies were in such great shape that it was an eye-popping show. It takes years of training and dedication to the sport to even get to the competition stage. During the twelve to sixteen weeks before the show, there is intense training and a strict diet plan they fit around their everyday lives. The preparation in the final week, to make sure their bodies look their absolute best, includes hair removal and layers of self-tanning. The whole process takes a very special kind of person, someone who is brave, dedicated, focused, driven, strong-minded and consistent to name a few characteristics.

All these qualities are needed to achieve your dreams and goals, whatever they may be. Brian's dream carried on a little longer, as he won a place in the finals in a few weeks. You, too, have what it takes to achieve your goals. It's all within you!

27 July

Teamwork makes the dream work! I have the privilege of working with some of the most amazing women and men you could ever wish to meet, building lasting friendships and having fun along the way. When you involve others in anything you do, not only does it happen quicker, but it is also such much more enjoyable. Teamwork makes the dream work.

Helping others is also a huge part of teamwork. By helping others, you learn so much more. Whether your team is for work or leisure, surrounding yourself with like-minded people is key. Having a team means you never have a weakness, because everyone brings to the table what they are good at. Your team could be family, friends, or at work. Value everyone in your team, because everyone has a place. Teamwork makes the dream work!

28 July

I am what I am!
And what I am needs no excuses.
I deal my own deck,
Sometimes the aces, sometimes the deuces.
It's my world that I want to have a little pride in,
My world and it's not a place I have to hide in.
Life's not worth a dam till you can shout out.

Mark Owens

This is a classic song by Gloria Gaynor. It's one of my favourites and one I remind myself of when I am ever knocked or put down. When you have a bubbly personality and a happy and cheery disposition, people can bring you down. Years ago, I used to let it get to me. Now, however, I don't, as I enjoy being me. "I am what I am." Once you know who you are and what makes you tick, you start to have fun. And when we have fun, the whole world has fun with us!

29 July

Are you an "and then some" person? Do you give 10 percent more than expected? Amazing things happen when you do. If you take away ten percent of the average man's height, you have a short man. If you add 10 percent to his height, you have a giant!

Nowadays, people's expectancy level is not very high, so if you give an extra 10 percent, you both will feel good. Not only are you spreading goodwill, great things come back to you in return. Try it! I make it my daily purpose to give an extra 10 percent in all I do. If nothing else, it makes you feel great!

Give 10 percent extra today.

30 July

On the tube yesterday, a man's bag had two buttons on it which looked like eyes, a strap that looked like a nose, and the bottom of the bag was curved. So the bag looked like a smiley face! My colleague thought I was mad.

What simple things make you smile? Are you looking for things to make you smile and be happy, or do you walk around looking for things that upset or offend you. Every day I see things that make me smile, however simple they may be. It's amazing what you can see when you start looking.

31 July

The fourteenth Dalai Lama (the spiritual leader of Tibet) once said,

> I'm sure we all feel the same about the troubles in the world and consequently pretty helpless. But you see, in reality, we only have control over ourselves.

> If we are at peace with ourselves and pass this feeling onto others, eventually it will have an enormous affect and far beyond that which we dare to believe.

Have a peaceful day.

1 August

Do you sometimes find it difficult to make decisions? Usually we try to make a decision without all the facts and before we actually need to. Then we panic about it. Firstly, calm down. The mind works better when it's relaxed. Start gathering all the facts about the matter in question, and don't make a decision until you have to. While you gather all the information, the mind starts to sort out the answer. So when the time comes to make that decision, it generally makes itself. I now find most of the decisions I need to make happen naturally and in good time, without any stress or worry.

2 August

Mother Teresa said,

> People are often unreasonable, illogical and self-centred—forgive them anyway. If you are kind, people may accuse you of selfish ulterior motives—be kind anyway. If you are successful you'll win some unfaithful friends and some genuine enemies—succeed anyway. If you're honest and sincere, people may deceive you—be honest and sincere anyway. What you spend years creating, others could destroy overnight—create anyway. If you find serenity and happiness, some may be jealous—be happy anyway. The good you do today, will often be forgotten—do good anyway!
>
> Give the best you have and it will never be enough—give the best you have anyway. In the final analysis, it's between you and God; it was never between you and them anyway!

3 August

Do you have a dream? Something you want to achieve in life, some big goal, or something you feel you want but think you may not be able to achieve? The inspirational people in life say you can achieve anything you put your mind to. They have usually achieved their dreams and goals and do believe anyone can do the same with the correct thinking, attitude, and a bit of determination.

How can we possibly believe we can do it when we haven't yet done it? Well, it all starts with blind faith. There are plenty of people who can and will encourage us, and that's just what we need. So surround ourselves with these people, not the non-believers. Anyway, what have we got to lose? If it doesn't work, we've lost nothing. And when it does work, we can then inspire others to achieve, and the inspiration goes forward. Dream a dream and have the blind faith attitude that it will work.

4 August

I read a book some years ago called *The Perfect Present*. It wasn't about a gift for someone; it was talking about living in the present moment. It's strange, but as human beings, we live our lives in the past and in the future, paying less attention to the present. We sometimes look at the past with regrets, but the past is there to learn from. The future may be of concern, but we haven't gotten there yet. The only reality we have is the present. So if we do our very best today, our past will be full of joy, and a happy future is assured.

Let's try, just for today, to live in the present, and do the same tomorrow and beyond.

5 August

I've just been to Dallas and spent the last five days in the most amazing company of the top Mary Kay directors. I have been surrounded by inspiring and positive people and energised by the whole process. With these people, could you imagine feeling the same?

Conversely, if we spend time with negative people, we feel drained, tired, and totally unmotivated. The same happens when we hear or read the news. Yes, we have to be informed, but that's as far as it goes. It's so important to surround ourselves with positivity and stay away from negativity. If we are strong, we can help ourselves and, consequently, help others. That is what life's all about. We owe it to ourselves, and we owe it to others.

Stay positive, and surround yourself with positive people.

6 August

There are simple sayings that go, "To attract a friend you need to be one first," and, "To give love, firstly love ourselves." In other words, we can't give what we don't have. If we want to influence people, which we all do in some shape or form, we have to work on ourselves first, so we can be an example to others. There are so many people who need guidance, and it's up to those with the strength and purpose of mind to help others achieve their goals and aspirations. Let's spend today being a friend to someone and a day loving ourselves.

7 August

I really feel I have spent the past few days visualising and have captured a vision of how I am shaping my life. Having a vision is so powerful and so important, as it gives us a direction to move forwards.

V   Claim the victory: act as if you're already there.

I   Integrity: act with purpose and imagination, because it all begins in the imagination.

S   Serve: give of yourself to others daily.

I   Influence: be true to yourself, and you will influence others.

O   Obstacles: signs you are moving in the right direction.

N   Never, never give up!

Capture your vision of how you want to shape your life.

8 August

"The reason I can do the things I can, and you can't do the things you can't, is because I think I can, and you think you can't." I heard that powerful statement a while ago. This, for me, is the fundamental reason some people do and some people don't!

I remember when my son was four years old, he'd climbed onto the shed roof as he wanted to fly round the garden like a bird. After a brief discussion, on my instruction he was to jump—I knew I would catch him. As he landed I my arms he said "see mummy—I did it!" He believed he could fly.

Can you, or can't you. The choice is yours!

9 August

You would think the oyster wouldn't seem to have much going for it. It's an unattractive creature, living in the silt at the bottom of the sea. Yet it is capable of providing great beauty.

Even having a thick shell doesn't stop irritations getting into the oyster's protected world. When it cannot get rid of them, it uses the irritations to do the loveliest thing. If there are irritations in our life today, there is only one prescription: make a pearl! Well, if the oyster can do it.

The more we train ourselves to think of irritations, obstacles, and hiccups as a way of life and as being there to help us along our journey, the easier it gets to turn them into something positive. It's been said the greatest joys come from something negative or something you've had to put right. May you create pearls along your life's journey.

10 August

A wealthy businessman noticed a fisherman lounging on his boat, drinking a cup of coffee. "You're back pretty early," he said to the fisherman.

"I've caught enough fish already. I'm through for the day," said the fisherman.

"But it's not even noon," said the businessman. "You could go back out and catch more fish."

"Why should I do that?"

"If you catch more fish, you can sell more fish. If you sell more fish, you can make more money."

"Why would I want to do that?"

"Because if you made more money, you could buy a second boat, hire a crew, catch more fish, make even more money, and become rich, like me."

Again the fisherman asked, "Why would I want to do that?"

The businessman sighed. "So you're free to do whatever you want and treasure life."

The fisherman looked at the businessman and grinned. "But that's what I'm doing now!"

Do what you do, and do it well. Enjoy where you are now!

11 August

Never draw the curtain on the window of opportunity.

How many of us go through life blinkered by the world around us, never knowing its true beauty? Do we appreciate the amazing opportunities out there all day, every day? They just go unnoticed.

Never draw the curtain on the window of opportunity. Keep your options and eyes open, and keep an open mind. Opportunities will present themselves to you. Once you start to become aware of opportunities, they present themselves more often. And before you know it, you're looking for them daily.

12 August

"If friends were flowers, I'd pick you." "If every time I thought of you, I planted a flower, I would walk happily in my garden forever!"

Those are two wonderful sayings I've come across over the years. They came to me just now as I looked at two beautiful bunches of flowers given to me by two darling friends. Do you think of yourself as lucky to be able to choose your friends? Do you appreciate that people come into your life for a *reason*, a *season,* or a *lifetime*? Are you grateful to have someone special, flowers in your garden, that make you smile and help you know what it's like to be loved? Who are your flowers? Do they know how special they are?

13 August

"Come to the edge."

"We can't; we're afraid."

"Come to the edge."

"We can't; we will fall!"

"Come to the edge." And they came. He pushed them, and they flew!

I'm sure we've all felt like this. I know I have, often. But the really interesting thing is the times I've gone to the edge and was pushed, I *did* fly. Stepping out of our comfort zone—personal growth—is all related! Do that thing you're afraid of, however big or small, ask someone to be by your side, and I bet you anything you like, you'll fly! Be brave, have courage, have faith, and you will be amazed!

14 August

For some reason, we tend to base who we are on what we have. "If I have more money, I'm better." "If I only had this partner, all would be OK." "If I was able to do . . . , it would mean . . . ."

Life is one big ball of cookie dough. When we're born, God gives us twelve million cookie cutters. All we have to do is cut the bits we want, and guess what? Love is the oven! All we need to know is all we have is all we need. It's all within us!

We are always looking for something. Have you ever really stopped and looked around you? I know we need reminding. Please do, and I know we'll feel so much more comforted.

All you need is within you!

15 August

What do I have to be grateful for? It's something I hear a lot. I believe we mainly focus on what is not right in our lives. I hear people say, "My children are always arguing at home, my husband is always away working, and there is so much to do at home, I never have the time."

You can always find something to be grateful about. Every situation can be a source of opportunities. Look at it this way. How about being grateful for the fact you have children when some people can't. At least you have a home, a roof over your head. If your husband is away working, at least he has a job, and while he's away, you can spend time doing the bits you need to do at home. However simple and obvious it is, there is always something to be grateful for, whatever the situation.

Always look for the silver lining. It's there if you look hard enough. Take a moment now to think of something to be grateful for.

16 August

Yesterday we were reminded to look for the silver linings in every situation. Sometimes it's a real challenge but one that is so rewarding. Looking for good in all things can be fun, as is being grateful for all you have. When you've had a taxing day, to have an attitude of gratitude can sometimes be difficult, but it is essential. Someone once said, "At the end of each day, as you drift off to sleep, think of three new things you are grateful for". In the beginning, this will be easier, then as you run out of things to be grateful for, what you'll find yourself doing is looking, in each day, for new things to be grateful for so you have three new things to recall that night. Can you now see what's happening? We are now looking for the good in all situations and new things to be grateful for. Lives will be transformed.

Exciting! From experience, I can tell you it does work. And before you know it, it becomes a habit, and amazing things begin to happen. I am so grateful to you for reading this today. Thank you!

17 August

As the story goes, I lost my wallet one afternoon. You know the feeling of total helplessness. I had just been to the bank, so my wallet was full of cash, credit cards, and important papers. I was in panic mode! I drove back to all the places I had been that day: bank, supermarket, cleaners, petrol station. I retraced all my steps. Nothing! At 8.15 p.m., the doorbell rang. A nice young man stood there, smiling, with my wallet in his hand. He found it on the ground at the petrol station, sandwiched between the pumps. Right where I had reached to fill up my car. I couldn't speak.

He said returning it was an "easy decision." He saw my address on my driver's license, looked on a city map, and drove over thirty miles to my house. He lived in a different county. His only explanation was that was how he was brought up. I thanked him many times and offered him money in gratitude. He refused. He said the look on my face was worth the trip. He restored my faith in humankind, and it lasts to this day.

18 August

We all have routines that become habits. Our commute to work, for example. A man who had made the same trip for fifteen years had road works along his journey for a week and was forced to take a different route. He was not pleased and grumped about it for a while.

After a few days, something changed. In slow-moving traffic, he noticed an old barn for sale and thought, *Who would want to buy that old thing?* The next day, he studied the barn with more interest. And the next day, he pulled over and found himself looking around the old place, took the number of the estate agents, and booked a viewing. A couple of days later, he made an offer. He then spent every spare moment for the next two years working on his new project, a barn conversion.

Which routine could you flip in search of inspiration? Why not take a detour, and see what happens!

19 August

Do you ever look at the talents others and think, *I wish I could do that*? Maybe a dancer or singer you see on the television, an athlete winning a medal, or an artist creating wonderful pieces of artwork admired by many. Do you ever stop to think that maybe someone looks at you and thinks, *Wow I would love to be able to cook like Vanessa,* or, *I wish I was a talented speaker like Vanessa.*

We tend to concentrate on other people's talents rather than our own. If you have a talent, use it in every way possible. Don't hoard it. Don't dole it out like a miser. Spend it lavishly, like a millionaire intent on going broke.

What are your talents?

20 August

A man found a cocoon of a butterfly. He sat and watched the butterfly for several hours as it struggled to force its body through the little hole. Then it seemed to stop making any progress. It appeared as if it had gotten as far as it could, and it could go no further. Deciding to help, the man took a pair of scissors and snipped off the remaining bit of cocoon.

The butterfly then emerged easily. But it had a woollen body and small, shrivelled wings. The man continued to watch the butterfly, because he expected that, at any moment, the wings would enlarge and expand to support the body, which would contract in time. Neither happened. In fact, the butterfly spent the rest of its life crawling around with a swollen body and shrivelled wings. It was never able to fly.

What the man, in his kindness and haste, did not understand was that the restricting cocoon and the struggle required for the butterfly to get through the tiny opening were God's way of forcing fluid from the body of the butterfly into its wings, so it would be ready for flight once freed from the cocoon. Sometimes struggles are what we need to be able to fly!

21 August

Let's start thinking of ourselves as lifetime students at a large university. How we learn is our total relationship with the world we live in, from the moment we are born to the moment we die. Each experience is a valuable lesson to be learned. If we choose path A, we will learn one set of lessons. If we choose path B, we will learn a different set of lessons. If we take path A, we get to taste the apples. If we take path B, we get to taste the pears. If we hate both apples and pears, we can find another path. The trick is simply to make whatever place we're in our educational forum and learn everything we can about ourselves and the world around us. Whatever happens as a result of our decision, we'll handle it.

22 August

I learnt yesterday that to a stranger "I count." Yesterday, I met a remarkable woman called Anna, a foreign lady earning her way in life as an artist in a holiday location. What is so remarkable about her art is she creates the most amazing pictures by using coloured spray paints in a can. I asked her to create a special one for me, as I loved what she did and wanted to give her the work. I chose the colours and the style. I chose a lady with butterfly wings on a picturesque sunset with the odd, floating butterfly and the words, "It's your choice," at the top. She loved it so much, she got her colleague to take a photo of it.

She asked me why I chose what I did. I explained, "You can choose to be the cocoon or the butterfly."

Anna smiled and said, "Thank you for the lesson." With limited language so much can be said with a beautiful picture!

23 August

I saw my artist friend again yesterday, and she greeted me, "Ah, butterfly lady," and smiled. "I told my friends about your butterfly message. About having the choice, and they like it very much! Thank you again."

Wow! I was so excited, I couldn't wait to tell Brian, "She thinks my message is important! She told her friends." Something I feel so passionately about is now being passed around Spain. I love it! Just imagine if someone who hears the saying, "It's your choice," at just the right time in life. How massive that would be!

Never underestimate what you feel is important. If it is important to you, you own it with such passion it becomes powerful. Live with passion.

24 August

There must be hundreds, possibly thousands of people here at the beach, all having a wonderful time. For all these people, there are a handful of men and women selling what they can to make a living. Some are selling pirated DVDs; some selling sunglasses and watches. Some are offering hair braiding and others massages. Their services are turned down with a, "No, thank you." Some just say no or shake their head. Some don't make eye contact at all and just ignore them.

Most of these people say no in some way. Do you think that stops the vendors from trying? No! They keep asking. No doubt they'll be back tomorrow, asking again. They get more nos than yeses, but they don't quit, because there will always be someone who wants to buy, and they will find that person. Even though they can be annoying, you have to give them credit for keeping on and not taking no for an answer, and treating no as next.

25 August

We had a great conversation with a restaurant owner. Manjed used to be in pharmaceuticals in the United Kingdom and has owned his own restaurant in Spain for four years. He says, "Instead of helping ill people feel better with prescriptive medicine, I now do it with good food!"

Manjed is the proud owner of Leonardos', a great restaurant. He is so passionate about serving great food and wine as his preferred medicine now. He said his friends in the UK all seemed to be having so much more fun owning restaurants. He saw an opportunity in the Spanish tourist market, took it, and hasn't looked back.

Sometimes when we do something unexpected, it could be what we were meant to be doing all along. Manjed now uses his experience and knowledge from his pharmacy background with his love for food to create the perfect menu.

26 August

Feel the fear, and do it anyway! My ten year-old daughter is a bit of a worrywart, or so I thought. Yesterday we went to the water park and braved the boomerang. I told Liberty, "I'll go first, darling, so I'll be at the bottom when you get there." She was so desperate to experience the ride, but I knew it was an extreme drop and wanted to be there to console her when she landed at the end. It frightened me, but to my surprise, she loved every second of it! Even though she was fearful, she didn't want to look silly in front of the others. She rode it again with much enthusiasm.

It just goes to show if we do what we fear, it might not turn out too badly, and we might even enjoy the ride! Fear is *false evidence appearing real*, so we shouldn't let it stop us from doing what we want. Feel the fear, and do it anyway.

27 August

It starts with you! I have just read a fantastic book called *The Go Giver*. I was blown away by this story. One of the five key ingredients needed for giving is authenticity.

The author writes,

> People, remember this: no matter what your training, no matter what your skill, no matter what area you're in, *you* are the most important commodity. The most valuable gift you have often is *you*. As long as you're trying to be someone else, or putting on some act or behaviour someone else taught you, you have no possibility of truly reaching people. The most valuable thing you have to give people is yourself.

I really enjoyed reading this, as too many people feel they have nothing to offer. Everyone has something. It's true. How many times have we heard, "Just be yourself"?

Just be yourself, and enjoy being you.

28 August

My daily promise: I will continue to be inspired by the world around me and be constantly open to the possibilities of change every day.

Just as nature intended the cocoon to become the butterfly, I believe we all have the ability to transform to become the very best we can be!

As we dare to dream, and with energy, passion, and a loving and grateful heart, I believe in the magic of transformation.

You can have the life you choose: the cocoon or the butterfly. It's your choice!

What's your daily promise?

29 August

I have just been reminded of a remarkable story of a woman with breast cancer, whose treatment consisted of watching funny movies every day and repeating the words, "Thank you for my healing." Laughter and these five words were her daily medicine. She was so focused on making herself well, and in three months, she was completely clear, with no radiation or chemotherapy. Truly amazing!

It was also encouraging to know laughter really *is* the best medicine, and what we tell ourselves *does* have an effect on healing our bodies. Take a daily dose of humour, sprinkle with some healing words, and share with all around you! Have a healthy day.

30 August

There are three pans of boiling water, each on high fire. In the first pan are carrots, the second contains an egg, and coffee beans are in the third pan. After twenty minutes, the burners are turned off.

Each of these objects had faced the same adversity—boiling water—and each reacted differently. The carrot went into the water strong, hard, and unrelenting. After being subjected to boiling water, it softened and became weak. The egg had been fragile. Its thin, outer shell had protected its liquid interior, but after sitting in boiling water, its inside became hard. The ground coffee beans were unique, however. After they were in the boiling water, *they* had changed the water.

Which are you? When adversity knocks on your door, how do you respond? Do you go weak like the carrot, do you toughen up like the egg, or do you adapt and change the situation around you? May we all be coffee!

31 August

A son and his father were walking in the mountains. Suddenly, his son falls, hurts himself, and screams, "AAaaaaaaaahhhh!" To his surprise, he hears a voice somewhere in the mountains repeating, "AAaaaaaaaahhhh!" Curious, he yells, "Who are you?" He receives the answer, "Who are you?" He looks to his father and asks, "What's going on?"

The father smiles and says, "My son, pay attention." The father screams, "You are a champion." The voice answers, "You are a champion!" The boy is surprised but does not understand. Then the father explains. "People call this echo, but really this is life. It gives you back everything you say or do. Our life is simply a reflection of our actions. Life will give you back everything you have given to it."

Your life is not a coincidence; it's a reflection of you!

1 September

A blind boy sat on the steps of a building with a hat by his feet. He held up a sign which said, "I am blind, please help." There were only a few coins in the hat. A man walking by took a few coins from his pocket and dropped them into the hat. He then took the sign, turned it around, and wrote some words. He put the sign back, so everyone who walked by would see the new words. The hat soon began to fill up.

That afternoon, the man who had changed the sign came to see how things were. The boy recognised his footsteps and asked, "Were you the one who changed my sign this morning? What did you write?"

"I only wrote the truth," the man said. "I said what you said but in a different way. I wrote, 'Today is a beautiful day, but I cannot see it.'"

Be thankful for what you have. Be creative. Be innovative. Think differently and positively. The most beautiful thing is to see a person smile. Even more beautiful is knowing you are the reason behind it!

Think differently!

2 September

A group of frogs was travelling through the woods, and two of them fell into a deep pit. When the other frogs saw how deep the pit was, they told the two frogs they were as good as dead. The two frogs ignored the comments and tried to jump up out of the pit with all their might. The other frogs kept telling them to stop, they were as good as dead.

Finally, one of the frogs gave up. He fell down and died. The other frog continued to jump as hard as he could. Once again, the crowd of frogs yelled at him to stop the pain and just die. He jumped even harder, and finally made it out. When he got out, the other frogs asked, "Did you not hear us?" The frog explained he was deaf. He thought they were encouraging him the entire time.

An encouraging word to someone who is down can lift the person up and help him or her make it through the day. It is sometimes hard to understand the power of words. An encouraging word can go such a long way.

Special is the individual who will take the time to encourage another.

3 September

A group of school children were asked to list what they thought were the present seven wonders of the world. Though there were some disagreements, the following received the most votes: (1) Egypt's Great Pyramids, (2) Taj Mahal, (3) Grand Canyon, (4) Panama Canal, (5) Empire State Building, (6) St Peter's Basilica, (7) China's Great Wall.

While gathering the votes, the teacher noticed one student had not finished her list. So she asked the girl if she was having trouble. The girl replied, "Yes, a little. I couldn't quite make up my mind, because there are so many."

The teacher said, "Well, tell us what you have, and maybe we can help."

The girl read, "I think the seven wonders of the world are to see, to hear, to touch, to taste, to feel, to laugh, to love." The room was so quiet you could have heard a pin drop.

The things we overlook as simple and ordinary—and that we take for granted—are the most precious things in life. They cannot be built by hand or bought by humankind.

4 September

The story goes that some time ago, a man punished his three-year-old daughter for wasting a roll of gold wrapping paper to wrap an empty box as his Christmas present. He yelled at her, "Don't you know when you give someone a present, there is supposed to be something inside?"

The little girl looked up at him with tears in her eyes, and cried, "Oh, Daddy, it's not empty at all. I blew kisses into the box. They're all for you, Daddy." The father was crushed. He put his arms around his little girl and begged for forgiveness.

A short time later, an accident took the life of the child. It is also told that her father kept that box by his bed for many years, and whenever he was discouraged, he took out an imaginary kiss and remembered the love of the child who put it there.

We all have a gold container filled with unconditional love and kisses from our children, family members, and friends. Do we realise it is the most precious gift?

5 September

A man planted a rose and watered it faithfully. He saw the bud that would soon blossom but noticed thorns upon the stem. He wondered, *How can any beautiful flower come from a plant burdened with so many sharp thorns?* Saddened by this thought, he neglected to water the rose, and just before it was ready to bloom, it died.

So it is with many people. Within every soul there is a rose. We all have God-given talents as well as faults, and it is so important to water and nourish our talents so that the thorns diminish. If we concentrate on our thorns, we keep our talents from others.

Some people do not see the rose within themselves. One of the greatest gifts a person can possess is to be able to reach past the thorns of another and find the rose within. This is one of the characteristics of love, to look at a person, know their true faults, and accept that person into your life. Help others realise they can overcome their faults. If we show them the "rose" within themselves, they will conquer their thorns. Only then will they blossom many times over.

6 September

Going deeper. What do we leave behind in order to go deeper? Is there something deep within us that we haven't discovered yet? Always! However much we unravel, there will always be more to discover. How exciting!

What will it take for us to dig deeper? Do we need evidence something's there? Or do we just need to be curious enough? Do you want to know what lies within you? Do you want to go deeper and learn more about you? Seek and you will find. Don't get lost in the confusion on the surface. Go deeper, where it is calm and safe. Then share what you find, so you and others benefit from what you have to offer.

7 September

An elderly carpenter was ready to retire. He told his employer-contractor of his plans to leave the house-building business to live a more leisurely life with his wife and family. The contractor was sorry to see his good worker go and asked if he could build just one more house as a personal favour. The carpenter said yes, but over time, it was easy to see his heart was not in his work. He resorted to shoddy workmanship and used inferior materials. It was an unfortunate way to end a dedicated career.

When the carpenter finished his work, his employer came to inspect the house. Then ho handed the front door key to the carpenter and said, "This is your house. My gift to you." The carpenter was shocked! What a shame! If he had only known he was building his own house, he would have done it all so differently.

But you cannot go back. You are the carpenter, and life is a do-it-yourself project. Your attitude and the choices you make today help build the "house" you will live in tomorrow. Therefore, build wisely!

8 September

If I had a £50 note to offer you, you'd take it. If I screwed it up, you'd still want it. If I dropped it on the floor and ground mud into it, you'd still want it. No matter what I did to the money, you would still want it, because it did not decrease in value; it is still worth £50.

Many times in our lives we are dropped, crumpled, and ground into the dirt by the decisions we make and the circumstances that come our way. We feel as though we are worthless. But no matter what happened or what will happen, you will never lose your value. Dirty or clean, crumpled or finely creased, you are still priceless to those who love you. The worth of our lives comes not in what we do or who we know but by who we are.

You are special. Don't ever forget it!

9 September

We ask the doctor to fix our symptoms or complaints with medicine, forgetting that with most ailments, it's our mind that cures us, not medicine. Doctors have been known to use a sugar pill for mild symptoms and complaints, telling the patient it's medicine. Psychologically, the patient thinks it is something to fix his troubles. This is called the placebo effect.

It reminds us that the mind cures all.

10 September

The wise and wonderful Buddha once said, "A generous heart, kind speech, and a life of service and compassion are things which renew humanity."

I have been taught the Golden Rule: "Do unto others as you would have them do unto you." My mum always taught me to be kind to others if you want others to be kind to you, compliment others daily, look to do a good deed every day, and always be willing to act with love.

Bless my mum for teaching me such a valuable life lesson. I love you, Mum!

11 September

Take time to reflect on what you are grateful for in memory of 9/11 and write them here

12 September

Even though the events of 9/11 were catastrophic, once the initial shock of what happened sunk in, there was an amazing sight of community spirit. Firefighters who were helping to rescue people from burning buildings felt good, the people being rescued felt good, the onlookers felt good, and those of us watching on the television felt good. All these people were releasing serotonin, a feel-good enzyme in the brain. So even though we could do nothing to stop the events from happening, we could make a difference and try to make the best out of a truly bad situation.

Do something for someone today to make you both feel great, and pass it on!

13 September

Take care of your thoughts, because they become words. Your words then become your actions. Your actions become your habits. Your habits form your character. Your character forms your destiny. Your destiny will be your life.

All we do creates our lives. How do you want to live yours?

14 September

Beethoven's Story: Practice Makes Perfect

While critics thought Ludwig Van Beethoven's style of music was radical, the public absolutely adored his work. It's been said that after the performance of one of his original compositions, a group of well-wishers gathered around Beethoven to shower him with praise. One woman remarked that she wished God had bestowed her with such genius.

Beethoven replied, "It isn't genius, madam, nor is it magic. You can be as good as I am. All you have to do is practice on your piano eight hours a day for forty years."

Excellence is not an act but a habit. The things you do the most are the things you do the best. I think we simply forget that when we do something consistently, we get very good at it. And when we get good, we become more confident. And when we become confident, there is no stopping us!

15 September

Sitting here watching Liberty prepare for her grading in karate, I could see her getting more and more nervous. When I got the chance, I asked her why she looked nervous. I was sure she said earlier how confident she felt with all the practicing she had done. She replied, "I just found out we will be performing individually in front of everyone, and I thought we would be in a group."

I replied, "That's brilliant! Just think how proud of you Dad will be when he hears you performed on your own." My aim was to keep her focus on the end result, so she wouldn't worry too much about the grading. A smile crept across her face and as I hugged her. "I am so proud of you, darling. I just know how fantastic you'll be."

Liberty performed brilliantly and came away with top marks. Focus on the result you want, and prepare the best you can at each stage along the way.

16 September

What if you had a bank account in which every morning there were £86,400 in it? But what there was left at the end of the day was not carried over to the next. What would you do? You would spend every penny. We *do* have such a bank. It is called time!

We wake each morning to 86,400 seconds. If we looked at time as if it were money, we would spend it very differently. We tend to spend a lot of time planning how we spend a lot of money, but do we plan how we spend our time? Not always, or maybe not in too much detail. I'm sure we could get more out of our day if we planned how to spend our 86,400 seconds. Time is precious and a key part in building our futures.

17 September

According to legend, a nine-year-old boy and his mother went to a concert performed by the renowned pianist Ignacy Jan Paderewski. It was a very formal affair, and the boy was not impressed about being there. His mother wanted him to be a pianist. While waiting for the concert to begin, the boy was drawn to the piano on stage, so climbed onstage and began to play "Chopsticks." The crowd was irritated by the boy. Backstage, the pianist could hear the boy being booed by his audience. So he rushed out on stage, reached around the boy, and played a harmony to accompany the boy.

We hammer away on our projects, and when we are about to give up, the master comes along to help, whispering, "Keep going!" He improvises on our behalf, providing just the right touch at just the right moment. Keeping on keeping on, and the master will appear when you need him the most.

18 September

It was one of those days. The espresso machine was malfunctioning, the bakery had not delivered the bagels, someone from the morning shift called in sick, the crew from the previous evening failed to restock the cabinets with supplies, and there was a long queue waiting for their first cup of coffee for the day. A woman at the back of the line shouted, "What is taking so long? I don't have all day!"

"We are running on empty this morning," the manager said with a pleasant smile. He motioned for the woman to come forward. "What can I get for you?"

"I want a large coffee with steamed milk to go," barked the woman.

"Of course," said the manager. He looked past the woman to the other customers waiting in line and offered them a reassuring wink. Passing the woman her coffee and taking her money, he sent her on her way with a, "Have a nice day." The other customers stood silently, with confused looks. The manager said, "Folks, I'm really sorry for the inconvenience this morning. Because you have been so patient, *your* coffee is on the house."

19 September

Being popular has its advantages. But sometimes the recognition you receive has less to do with who you are and more to do with what you can do for others. An actor took his family away for the first time in months to spend uninterrupted quality time together. There were no phones ringing and no reporters hovering for interviews. One night, they decided to see a movie at the local theatre. As they took their seats, the twelve people who were already seated stood and cheered. The actor thought, *That's odd, I didn't think I had any fans in this part of the country.*

A man approached the actor and shook his hand. "I don't know who you are, but I sure am glad you and your family showed up," said the man. "You see, the theatre is only open one day a week. The manager said if we didn't get four more people in here, he wasn't going to run the film. I've been waiting to see this movie for two weeks, so I want to thank you for being here tonight."

20 September

It was the end of term and time for the final exam. The teacher made an interesting proposition to his students. "I know many of you do not like taking exams. If you are satisfied with your grade in this class up until now and are willing to have that as your final grade, you are free to skip the exam. I am completely serious," the teacher assured. Several students walked out of the room; three remained in their seats. "What is keeping you here?" he asked.

"I was hoping to use the final to get a better grade" said one student.

"I spent a great deal of time preparing for this exam. I'll be able to see how much I have learnt by taking the exam," said another student.

"I want to be totally satisfied," replied the final student.

"Well," said the teacher, "I have to say that you three have just passed one of life's biggest tests. Never settle for what is good enough when you want more. You are now excused. Each of you will receive an A!"

21 September

Miracles do happen. Two years ago, Brian was at the lowest point anyone could get to. Rock bottom felt like a good place to be. He was lower than that. Then two days ago, he achieved a lifelong dream. He won fourth place in the British Body Building championships! A true winner. Just to get to the final was an achievement! He truly has grown from zero to hero and in only two and one-half years! Through sheer dedication, focus, determination, persistence, and commitment, a miracle happened. A real-life story to prove to all of us miracles really do happen.

If you have clarity on what you want and believe, it will happen. What miracle is destined to happen for you?

22 September

What is your self-worth? The cost of the oils and the brushes that an artist uses to paint a picture has little to no relation to the value of the finished product. An artist could sell a painting for £43 million, and it would have nothing to do with the oils or the brushes he used but everything to do with *how* he used them. How do you use your talents? You could have two footballers; one could be worth millions of pounds and the other thousands of pounds. What's the difference? The one worth millions would be the key player in the team, score the goals, pass accurately, and so on. He has mastered his talents.

You are unique and worth so much more than you think! It has to start with *self-worth* and then others will value you more! What is your self-worth?

23 September

Following in from yesterday, are you starting to realise your self-worth? Here's a little task for you. Ask three people who love you to tell you what it is about you that they love. Is it your cooking, or your ability to make people laugh? Maybe you have a great smile. Do you put other people before yourself? Are you great with children? Maybe you give the best hugs! Ask them to be specific and to give it some great thought. They'll find it easy, I guarantee you!

When you have all their comments back, read them to yourself, saying, "I am" rather than "She is." You will be amazed at what others see in you! You might just find a reason to believe in yourself more, and you will definitely realise you are more unique than you think. To the world you are one person, but to one person you are the world!

24 September

I have always loved nature. The beauty and splendour that surrounds us each day never ceases to amaze me. Do we stop to realise just how wonderful nature is? Or do we ever think of nature as the purest example of how the world works? When I felt the lowest of the low and escaped in panic to clear my head, as I was frightened I would do something I'd regret, I sat in my car, looking through tear-filled eyes at the most amazing sunset. How could I not see a way forward when something as beautiful as that sunset happens with such little effort? Then it came to me. The nature I had grown to love and adore just happens and evolves effortlessly.

Could I help myself by tuning in to nature? By being clear about who I am and what I want? If nature can do it, so can I!

25 September

The only survivor of a shipwreck was washed up on a small, uninhabited island. He prayed every day to be rescued. A long while later, he managed to build a little hut from driftwood. One day after hunting for food, he arrived back to see his hut in flames, smoke rolling into the sky. He felt the worst had happened and had now lost everything. He was stunned by disbelief and anger, He cried out, "How could you do this to me?"

Early the next day, he was awakened by the sound of a ship approaching the island. It had come to rescue him! "How did you know I was here?" the weary man asked his rescuers.

"We saw your smoke signal," they replied.

The moral of the story: it's easy to get discouraged when things are going bad, but we shouldn't lose heart. Even in the midst of our pain and suffering, and remember when your "hut's on fire," things happen for a reason.

26 September

The other day, a friend confirmed for me, again, something I've always known to be true. My friend was a bit disturbed the other morning as he recalled his dream the evening before. "I've had the worse dream last night, and I've woken up feeling exhausted," he told me. He dreamt he'd been out drinking alcohol with his friends. My friend is in recovery from an addiction to alcohol, and has been now for a couple of years. He was very upset to have dreamt he'd been out drinking. The most amazing thing is he said, "I've got the most horrendous headache, and I feel hung-over!"

Apart from feeling bad for him, I felt really excited. If you go there in the mind, you'll go there in the body! In his mind he'd been drinking, so his body thought he had.

Never underestimate the power of the mind!

27 September

To succeed you have to believe in something with such a passion that it becomes a reality.

> Anita Roddick, Founder of The Body Shop

We often see success in our heads, and it is the best place to start, with a vision. However, to live the success, it has to be put into time and space, and involve others to become a reality. Then success is inevitable.

Believe with passion, and make it a reality.

28 September

Always aim higher than you believe you can reach. So often you'll discover that when your talents are set free by your imagination, you can achieve your goal. If people offer their help or wisdom as you go through life, accept it gratefully. You can learn much from those who have gone before you. But never be afraid or hesitate to step off the accepted path and head in your own direction, if your heart tells you it's the right way for you. Always believe you will ultimately succeed at whatever you do. And never forget the value of persistence, discipline, and determination.

You are meant to be whatever you dream of becoming.

29 September

Now I am no way the spider's biggest fan. Quite the opposite! But what I can't help being fascinated by is the spider's web. I nearly walked into one earlier, and it frightened the life out of me. That spider could have been my lunch, I was that close. I stopped to notice the spider was not resting in his web but weaving his home. The sunlight was shining perfectly onto the web for me to see even the tiniest detail. I could see him spinning his web and then moving around and around as he slowly finished in the middle.

Ono of my favourite sites is seeing the spider's web first thing in the morning as it collects dewdrops or on a frosty morning as they turn white. Magical. When was the last time we actually stopped to enjoy the view. It's all around us! Find something magical, and stop and appreciate it for a while. Have a magical day.

30 September

As I live each day, the more I realise the impact of attitude on life. Attitude, to me, is more important than facts. It is more important than the past, than education, than money, than circumstances, than failures, than successes, than what other people think, say, or do. It is more important than appearance, giftedness, or skill. It will make or break a company, a church, a home.

The remarkable thing is we have a choice every day regarding the attitude we will embrace for that day. We cannot change our past. We cannot change the fact people will act in a certain way. We cannot change the inevitable. The only thing we can do is play on the one string we have, and that is our attitude. I am convinced life is 10 percent what happens to me and 90 percent how I react to it.

And so it is with you. We are in charge of our attitudes.

1 October

You are my sunshine, my only sunshine.
You make me happy when skies are gray.
You'll never know dear, how much I love you.
Please don't take my sunshine away.

Jimmie Davis

I love this song and sing it to my kids when I want to cheer them up. I've sung it to them since they were babies, and now they still, aged ten and seven, stop when they hear this song.

Who is your sunshine? And whose sunshine are you? The best way to cheer yourself up is to cheer somebody else up. As autumn sets in and we prepare ourselves for the winter months, it is still so important to be the sunshine in people's lives.

You are my sunshine; shine on today.

2 October

A pencil maker told the pencil five important lessons just before putting it in the box.

- Everything you do will always leave a mark.
- You can always correct the mistakes you make.
- What is important is what is inside of you.
- In life, you will undergo painful sharpenings which will only make you better.
- To be the best pencil, you must allow yourself to be held and guided by the hand that holds you.

We all need to be constantly sharpened. This parable may encourage you to know that you are a special person, with unique God-given talents and abilities. Only you can fulfil the purpose you were born to accomplish. Never allow yourself to get discouraged and think your life is insignificant and cannot be changed. And like the pencil, always remember the most important part of who you are is what's inside you.

3 October

A blind girl hated herself because she was blind. She hated everyone, except her loving boyfriend. He was always there for her. She told her boyfriend, "If I could only see the world, I would marry you." One day, someone donated eyes to her. Weeks later, when the bandages came off, she was able to see everything, including her boyfriend.

He asked her, "Now that you can see the world, will you marry me?" The girl looked at her boyfriend and saw he was blind. The sight shocked her, and the thought of looking at them for the rest of her life led her to refuse his marriage proposal. Her boyfriend left with a broken heart.

A few days later, she received a note from him. It said, "Take good care of your eyes, my dear, for before they were yours, they were mine."

Be really careful what we ask for, as we may just get it.

4 October

Always remember, no matter what your training and no matter what your skills, you are the most important asset. The most valuable gift you have to offer is you! Pursuing any goal in life takes 10% knowledge and skill. The other 90% is people skills.

What is the foundation of people skills? Liking others? Caring for others? Being a good listener? All very admirable, but it's actually who you are. It all starts with you. When we try to be someone else, or behave like someone else, we will not truly reach people. The most valuable thing you have to give others is yourself. Whatever it may be you're selling, you're only selling yourself.

If you want people skills, be your own true self.

5 October

Remember, today is the tomorrow you worried about yesterday. And was it as bad as you thought? Probably not. Worry doesn't take away your troubles for tomorrow; it takes away your strength for today. A harvest starts with a seed. A fire starts with a spark. A storm starts with a raindrop. So our worries start small and then take over as they escalate.

Pretend you have a magic wand that can eliminate worry, and when your little worries escalate and overwhelm you, use your magic wand to turn them into little ideas or thoughts that escalate into big ideas and dreams.

That's turning worry on its head.

6 October

I was inspired yesterday by one woman's story. After having a nervous breakdown fifteen years ago from working in the rat race, Jane decided to change what she did for a living. Being in the corporate world had made her so unwell. She started a business in direct sales and became very successful over eight years of hard work. But something was still missing.

Jane's passion was fundraising for charities, her direct sales business, and bright and funky handbags.

Someone told her, "To change your results, you must change your focus." Overnight her new business was born. Selling bright and funky handbags. She now has everything in one place, and doesn't have to work quite so hard. She imports these fabulous bags to retail, and by doing so, she is able to help lots of charities. She earns more money than she ever thought possible, and there is no sign of another breakdown.

To change your results, you must change your focus.

7 October

Do you ever have one of those days where you're weighted down by day-to-day life? Then the simplest of things snaps you out of it and makes you concentrate on what really matters? The kids and I play a word association game. You say a word, and the next person says the first thing that comes to his or her mind. Jodi and I had a game before he went to bed, and it went something like this: diamond—jewels—sparkle—girls. Jodi's said, "Baby," I replied, "Miracle," and seven-year-old Jodi responded, "You!" Bless him.

I asked, "What made you say me? Why am I a miracle?"

"Because you work hard, you treat us to things, and you always kiss me goodnight."

Amazing, isn't it, what kids think miracles are! Needless to say, he made my overwhelming day worth it!

Thank you, Jodi. You are my miracle!

8 October

It's one thing to know you're going into a challenging season. You get prepared for it. You get mentally ready. But what about the difficulties we don't see coming? The unexpected crisis that catches us off-guard? Sometimes, it can seem so overwhelming that it almost knocks the wind right out of us.

We shouldn't be surprised by fiery trials. The forces of darkness would not be fighting against you if they didn't know there is something amazing in your future. Those unexpected difficulties are sometimes just signs you're on the right track. It's always darkest just before the dawn appears. The enemy always fights the hardest when you are closest to your breakthrough. The key is to stay the course, and keep fighting the good fight of faith. Keep your joy, and keep your focus on your future. You will overcome every obstacle and defeat every enemy.

9 October

Doing what you have to do now and having the discipline to do it means you are able to do what you want to do in the future! Have the courage to expand your thoughts, to stretch your talents, and to have a vision of the future no one will ridicule. Be grateful for your friends who mentor you, direct you, and share experiences with you! Feel blessed every day by the wonders that surround you, all day, every day. Enjoy what you do, and give it all you have, so you know you have made the most out of every situation.

All your hard work and efforts today will pay you back in the future. That you can be sure of! Do what you have to do now, and I have the discipline to do it, and you will be able to do what you want in the future!

10 October

After spending a weekend at Euro Disney with friends, it made my friends and I think about the magic involved in creating such a place. Kids and big kids alike are amazed and entertained by the magic of Disney. One man created his dream, and his dream lives on, as people want so much to believe magic exists today.

Magic! There could be so many meanings for magic, but this one expresses how we felt this weekend: *Memories are gifts I'll cherish.* What does magic say to you?

11 October

While standing in the queue at the Eurostar in Disneyland Paris, we chatted with a lady who explained her weekend away with her family was paid for by the charity Starlight, because her daughter is poorly. To reduce stress as much as possible, Starlight paid for everything, from travel to hotels in London, on both ends of their trip.

For this family, life is a day-to-day struggle, so support from a charity such as Starlight to provide light relief in the shape of Euro Disney is a true blessing. For those of us who are able to pop to Disney whenever we like, it is a great reminder to appreciate and be grateful for *all* we have, and wherever possible, to help charities like Starlight.

12 October

Look back and get experience. Look forward and see hope. Look around and find reality. Look within and find yourself. Over the past few years, I have spent lots of time, money, and energy on self-development. I believe when we develop ourselves, we become better people and more interesting to be around.

I will always enjoy developing as an individual, but I have found the most rewarding thing I have done and found most strength from is looking deep within myself and connecting to my inner being. Some people call it the Source. Whatever you want to call it, take time today to search within yourself. Be still and quiet, and imagine the energy around you vibrating further and further away from you, until you can no longer see it and are connected to a light. This is where the magic happens, and we can feel so connected nothing else matters.

Take time today to find yourself!

13 October

Is it possible your identity is a result of what happened to you in the past? Is it possible your true self feels like it has been buried by your identity? Do you sometimes feel like you play two parts in your daily life? Today, be aware of when you play a part and when you are truly you. I bet you see a difference. Granted, there are times we play a part to help us in a given situation. True happiness comes from being who we are born to be daily. True peace comes from knowing your being is making a difference in this world.

Spend a moment today to see your true being.

14 October

As a result of writing this book, I created a brand called Be a Butterfly, because I believe we all have the choice to be the cocoon or the butterfly! My wonderful and talented sister-in-law wrote this poem for me. Thank you, Trudie, for summarising the simplicity of transformation!

Be a Butterfly!

A butterfly has beauty, that we cannot compare,
An example of God's finest work, his most creative flair.
A butterfly has freedom to go where its heart desires,
An energy unending, it rarely ever tires.
A butterfly transforms itself, striving to get it right
Through a cycle of improvement, 'til perfection is in sight.
A butterfly has strength, spending long spells in the air,
Yet floats by, like a feather we hardly know is there.
So many amazing qualities, we really all should try
To transform ourselves and our lives and Be a Butterfly!!

15 October

Change! Change happens all the time. We are where we are today as a result of continuously changing. _C_hoose to create _h_abits and to take _a_ction with a _n_ever-ending belief and a _g_iving heart, and _e_mbrace the change with _e_nergy and _e_nthusiasm! What other choice do you have?

16 October

Cherish your friends. Did you know your friends are like ivy? Ivy sticks to you, no matter what the weather. It hides the patches you don't want others to see and the holes where something is missing. There also comes a time when you feel you're falling apart and could collapse to the ground. Then you realise it's the ivy that is holding you together!

I have a friend who is my ivy. I didn't realise she was my ivy until I had the strength to see past where I was. She held me together when all I could do was exist. Since then, I view her through very different eyes. I see my ivy as a companion and a support, and not an addition.

Are we ivy ourselves or to others, or an addition? Cherish all friendships.

17 October

Do what you love, and love what you do! That's what my dad always told me.

Ever since the day I was laughed at in front of a room full of my peers at school, Dad said to me, "Mum and I only want you to be happy. We don't care about what grades you get in school, but what we do care about is that you spend your life doing what makes you happy." I appreciate he was trying to make me feel better about being laughed at, but at the time, I was heartbroken!

The same message was repeated throughout my childhood, so when it came to choosing how I wanted my life to look and how I wanted to earn a living, Dad's words rang loud and clear.

Thanks, Dad, as now I am living my dream life, because I do what I love and love what I do!

18 October

"How does one become a butterfly?" she asked.
"You must want to fly so much that you are willing to give up being a caterpillar!"

Trina Paulus

I have found this to be one of the biggest blocks that prevents people from moving forward. It is scary to leave behind what we know as our reality and step into the unknown. A quote from the wonderful Hans Christian King comes to mind: "To have faith is to believe without seeing. When jumping off a cliff in faith, we have the biggest parachute in the world." Hard to do at times, but extremely rewarding! Just think of how you would feel when you step out in faith into the unknown and get the result you want. What a story it would make.

It's OK to be afraid as long as your courage outweighs your fear. Sometimes we have to forget the reasons why we can't do something and concentrate on why we can. Focus on the success that comes as a result of having the courage!

Let go and fly!

19 October

How does a blind man learn how to let go? This was a question I asked myself after watching a blind man cross a busy road. I don't know about you, but when I was younger and first learnt to cross the road, I felt nervous about crossing bigger and busier roads on my own. And I have my sight.

So how does a blind man, with only a white stick, cross a busy road? He has to let go of any fears and trust! Trust the drivers will see his white stick and see a blind man crossing the road, and trust the drivers have their wits about them and are concentrating on the road ahead. Have you ever tried to walk about, even for a small amount of time, with your eyes closed? It is not a comfortable feeling. Some people don't have a choice.

If I blind man can let go of his fears and trust, why can't we?

20 October

Unexpected inspiration. Don't you feel so much more empowered when you are inspired when you least expect it? Films do this for me. I don't watch many films, but when I do, I am always inspired by the lesson I learn from watching others act out a story. *The Green Mile,* starring Tom Hanks, truly inspired me to think differently about how others see us, and as long as we are content with who we are, it shouldn't matter how others see us.

The Green Mile is about final days on death row and how the inmates learn, as their lives comes to an end, to ask for forgiveness for the crimes they have committed and feel peace. The prison officers play a huge part in helping them find peace in their final days. Tom Hanks, the chief officer, learns one of the prisoners is innocent. They become very close as Tom Hanks's character learns true forgiveness and peace as he watches his new friend transform the lives of others with his powers. His new friend dies on death row an innocent man; the only crime he committed was to love humanity and own his peace. He died a happy man.

21 October

Logic makes us think. Emotion makes us act! I'm not sure if I have heard truer words said. How many times have we heard things or seen something that makes us think?

But how many times has that been coupled with emotion to actually make you act on your thoughts? Not many, probably. We see and hear things all the time that make us think differently, but rarely are they coupled with emotion that makes us actually act on our thoughts!

May you be blessed today to experience something or someone that makes you act on your emotion!

22 October

We just arrived home from an incredible week in Memphis, Tennessee, the home of Elvis Presley. A group of us travelled together and shared the story of the King of Rock and Roll. Whether you are a fan of Elvis Presley or not, the one thing that has to be admired about this phenomenal man is the fact that as a small child, he always knew he was destined for great things. From very humble beginnings, born into a poor family, he always had a passion for music. How can one man make such a difference?

Being different is not always a bad thing, but having a passion and a belief are always great things Surely, Elvis Presley proves to us that all things are possible!

There is only one you. "The Wonder of You"!

23 October

Written by Elvis Presley for his dad, Vernon.

I not only live for today but for the day after today. I have pursued my vision and reached the mountaintop, but the peak of a mountain can be a lonely place. I want to thank you for understanding. I learned early in life that only by filling my existence with an aim, could I find an inner peace. I want to thank you for giving me intangible gifts. You gave me gifts from your heart—understanding, tolerance and concern. You gave me gifts of your mind—purpose, ideas, and projects. You gave me gifts of your words—encouragement, empathy, and solace. Respect is avid; it wants to contain everything and to retain everything. To you my father—my friend—my confidante, I have an avid respect. Thanks for always being near the top of the mountain when I needed you.

24 October

The plate spinner has definitely mastered the act of staying in control of more than one thing at any a time. How much practice would it take to spin many plates and keep your eye on them all so they didn't fall and smash? Much practice, and I bet he still has the odd broken plate!

I'm sure we all sometimes feel a bit like that with our daily lives and all we have to do from day to day, keeping all our plates spinning at any one time and then keeping our eyes on them all to keep them from smashing. When I was reminded of the plate spinner, I didn't feel too bad. Occasionally we will drop one. It happens!

As we know, life is a balancing act and definitely a work in progress. Keep spinning, and the balance will become easier.

25 October

A wise man once told me; Life doesn't always give you what you want but sometimes gives you what you need to grow. At times this is just what we need to hear. When it all gets a bit much and you feel perhaps nothing is going to plan, or maybe something happens that rocks your world, it's worth remembering that maybe it's part of the plan to make you grow and become stronger.

When we see it from this angle, it sure makes us feel a bit better. In that case, give me what I need to grow, because I know it wouldn't happen to me if I wasn't able to cope.

Take what life gives you and grow.

26 October

Not to have a care in the world! How lovely!

I picked my seven-year-old son up from his friend's house today, and he was bouncing around on a trampoline in his T-shirt and pants! To be fair, it was a beautiful October afternoon. He was underdressed because they had been for a walk in the woods, and Jodi covered himself, his boots, his jeans, and his jacket in mud! He had an amazing time rolling about in the mud with his friend and bouncing around on a trampoline.

I washed him down in the bath, fed him his tea, and tucked him into bed. No doubt he'd do it all again tomorrow. Maybe we should treat ourselves to a day like this! Do exactly what we want and do it without a care in the world.

See you in the woods. I'll be the one rolling around in the mud.

27 October

"Make me feel important." Have you ever spent the day imagining everyone you saw was wearing a sandwich board that said, "Make me feel important." It's actually really good fun, whether you compliment them, hold a door open for them, let them go before you on a roundabout, or simply smile so they know they have been noticed. I tend to make it a continuous habit to acknowledge people with a smile, a hello, or maybe a compliment about how lovely they look.

I had never thought too much of it, until a girlfriend told me they miss me and my happy gestures at school in the mornings. "It's just not the same anymore" she said, "especially in the mornings, when everyone is always rushing about."

You never know what a difference your actions will make to someone. Try to make everyone you meet today feel important. Thank you for reading this. You are fantastic.

28 October

I'm sure you know the story of the golden egg, but it bears repeating. A man finds a golden egg in the nest of his goose. To his delight, there is one there every day. The man became greedy the richer he became. So he thought he would get all the eggs at once and be done with it. So he cut the goose open and found nothing!

Be grateful each day for what you have. Otherwise, you may find one day it's all gone. Live for today, and we will be richer in so many ways.

29 October

Oh, to have the mindset of a child! Jodi pensively asked me the other day, "Mummy, if someone has no money and they find a 1pence piece on the ground, that's the first step to one million pounds, isn't it?"

"Yes, darling. Why do you ask?

"I just wanted to know that however big something seems, as long as I make a start, I'm well on my way and can begin my journey." How profound for a seven-year-old boy!

Why is it that as we grow older, we can lose sight that making the first step in any journey is the most important step to make? We are sometimes so frightened by the enormity of a journey that we don't even begin.

Thank you, Jodi, for asking this question of me and reminding us how important it is to take the first step of a journey, however big or small it may seem.

Take the first step on your journey as if you were an excited child again.

30 October

The colour of heartache. A schoolteacher asks her class, "What is the colour of heartache?"

The children all have different answers. "Orange, the colour of sunsets, of endings," says one.

"Silver, the colour of sharp blades, stabbing at your insides," says another.

"Blue, the colour of woeful music."

"Green, the sign of new growth, new beginnings."

"Red, the colour of blood; broken hearts bleed."

"Dull grey, the colour of heavy lead, weighing down your body."

"Purple, the colour of tender bruises."

"Pearl white, the colour of gnawing teeth."

"Black, the colour of darkness."

"Yellow, the colour of festering sores."

As the children answer, the teacher sits at her desk, drawing with pastels, choosing the colours her class speaks. When the class has run out of ideas, the teacher shows them her drawing. With their words of heartache, she has drawn a rainbow.

Everyone's journey is so different! But together it creates the most beautiful picture!

31 October

Problems occur when we do not know our true selves. Conflicts and arguments can happen, and day-to-day life can feel like an uphill struggle. When we are in tune with our values, the values that are important to us, we live our lives accordingly. This brings peace and harmony to our daily lives.

Stay true to you to create the life you want for yourself. Know who you are, and stay true to yourself!

1 November

A long time ago, there was a story of a rich man in search of peace, pleasure, and happiness, so he set off around the world to find it. He raced around, hiring planes and boats to get him around the world as quickly as he could. He was in such a rush he failed to notice the seasons and cultures around the world, the people, and the nature that is our beautiful planet.

On the rich man's deathbed, a wise man said to him, "What a journey you have been on. Did you find what you were looking for?"

"No," said the rich man.

"I didn't think so," said the wise man. "In your haste to race round the world to find what you were looking for, you whizzed past it without realising it was there all along."

2 November

Happiness isn't just a random feeling; happiness is a choice! It's a decision we have to make by an act of our will. Throughout life, you'll have plenty of opportunities to lose your joy. We all go through disappointments; we all have times when things don't go our way. It's very easy to let the circumstances of life make us bitter and dejected as we go through the motions of day-to-day living. But if you're going to live in victory, if you're going to thrive the way you were intended, you've got to make the decision that you're going to enjoy life. You've got to choose to be happy in spite of circumstances every single day.

Today, remember, this is the day that you have created. Choose to enjoy and be glad in it! As you choose joy, you are tapping into the power of strength which will carry you through to victory all the days of your life!

3 November

This time of year it's very easy to get caught up in all sorts of preparations for this, that, and the other. Organising families and holiday celebrations, parties, and shopping for all. Sometimes we can get a bit overwhelmed. Tonight we took Liberty and two friends to a children's music concert for her tenth birthday. She would not let me sit down. What fun!

I have definitely come home more relaxed, having sung my heart out and danced the night away. This will surely be my medicine from now on or my tonic for relaxing.

You know the saying: "Sing your song and dance like no one's watching!" So next time you feel you need to, play your favourite song and dance your dance!

4 November

Hope has three relatives: *willingness* to accept whatever comes knowing you'll come through stronger; *determination,* the ability to stand firm while those around you are falling; and _insight_ to see the character-developing hand that guides you.

As long as we have the willingness to take on whatever comes our way, the determination to keep taking it all on, and the insight to know if we stand strong we'll be all right, we will be great. Have hope today!

5 November

Isn't it crazy that the simplest and silliest things can make you smile? I was following a lorry yesterday. They tend to make me nervous, as you can't see anything in front of you but the back end of the lorry. However, this lorry was different. On the underside of the lorry was something like a cylinder or a drum of some sort, and just above the cylinder were two squares next to each other. To my delight, these shapes made a happy face wearing sunglasses! A pensive state transformed into a giggle, and I found myself smiling all the way home, because something so simple but silly tickled my fancy.

What will you find today that is so simple and so silly that you can't help smile or laugh out loud? I bet you find loads of things! Have a fun time looking for them.

6 November

Accept that where you are right now is exactly where you are meant to be. I have a friend who, for the past nine and one-half years has been hit time after time by challenge after challenge. She has two beautiful daughters, one who is poorly yet undiagnosed. She has struggled at times to venture out her front door. Hospital is their second home, and operations are the norm. This little girl is one of the most delightful children you could ever hope to meet, as is her big sister. My friend has lost her marriage, so she is a new, single mum, managing better than ever.

Though her trials are ongoing, she will always say to you how grateful she is to have a roof over her head, the ability to grow and become stronger, and two beautiful girls. It has also been suggested to her she writes a book to help others like her, and she will do a great job!

My friend has always said she has learnt to accept that where she is right now is exactly where she is meant to be!

7 November

It's never too late! Why do we sometimes feel that we are over the hill, too old to start something new? Could it be that all our lives have been about working towards or building our picture? When we think about it like that, aren't we then in the best place to start or create something we've always wanted to? We know life's experiences create our life and guide our pathways. So it is never too late, and there is never a right time. *You* create both! Do it now, and give others the benefit of your life's experiences.

My dad, in his sixties, has done just that. He's just published his first book—a lifelong dream of his! Admired by many and a role model for many more, we will all benefit now from his life's experiences.

8 November

Trust: you must trust that what you were born to be, you will be! *Train* yourself to be open-minded. The more open-minded you are, the more you will learn and grow. *Receive* and be open to all that you experience today will be your lesson for tomorrow. *Utilise* what you know so it can benefit others as well as yourself. *Share* what you have learnt with others, and more comes back to you. *Totally* rely on yourself, for you are the key to who you will become. To trust is not easy, but when you trust just a little, it all becomes a lot easier.

You must trust that what you were born to be, you *will* be!

9 November

Worry looks behind, sorry looks back, and strength looks forward. How true is this statement! Worriers are so focused on what's been before and places it in their future. They have taken their eyes off the ball, lost their focus, and let little things get in the way. When we're sorry, we tend to focus on what's been. Sometimes we dwell on what's happened and try to change a past event. Feeling sorry is very draining!

When you have a purpose, when you have a focus, when you feel in control, you focus forward and create your life as it was meant to be. You feel strong and determined. What a great way to feel! Don't worry about what's around you; don't feel sorry about what has been. Just stay focused on what lies ahead! Strength looks forward!

10 November

Coincidence, is there such a thing? Or is it synchronicity? In the dictionary, 'coincidence' says, "a remarkable concurrence of events or circumstances without apparent casual connection." This story proves that. Friends of my mum and dad's lost their son Bob. One day, Bob's mum had taken her granddaughter, Ava, Bob's niece, to the library for the afternoon. Ava was only two years old. She wandered around the library, as little ones do, stopped and picked out a book, Ava carried it to her grandma. To her surprise, the book was titled *The Day My Uncle Bob Died.* What are the chances of there being a book with that title and for Ava, age eighteen months, to pick it out. True synchronicity!

Wishing you a day of amazing coincidences and synchronicities.

11 November

"You Raise Me Up." This is not only a beautiful song, but the lyrics are uplifting. Do you have someone who lifts you up? "You raise me up, so I can stand on mountains, You raise me up, to walk on stormy seas. I am strong, when I am on your shoulders, You raise me up . . . to more than I can be." We all need someone in our life who, no matter what, is there for us. Someone to help us see the error of our ways or even be our stepping stone, our safety net when we fall. Who is this person for you? Who will raise you up to stand on mountains and help you be more than you can be? Be grateful for that individual!

12 November

What's important? Yesterday I witnessed a woman having a strong conversation with her work colleagues. She was being very firm and direct as she was getting her point across. It sounded very important and like it really mattered that her colleagues got it right or *her* neck was on the line.

Then her mobile rang. She politely excused herself and said she'd be back to finish her instructions. She answered the phone in a completely different tone. "Hello, sweetie, that sounds fabulous. Can you leave it by your bed for me, and when I kiss you goodnight later, I will be able to have a proper look? You clever girl. Love you, darling, sleep tight."

Clearly, this woman was wearing her mummy hat for this conversation. What was important to her was that her little girl knew she was the most important thing to her mummy, regardless of what was happening. What's important to you?

13 November

I was at a Christmas fayre yesterday, and one of the stallholders was dressed in green and red, and wearing a pair of reindeer antlers. She looked incredibly festive. Bless her, though, she had a face like thunder! Somehow she went from looking very festive to looking a bit daft. Had she been wearing a smile to match her outfit, she would have looked great. Instead, I got the impression her heart wasn't in it!

There is no point in looking the part if you are not going to act the part. It is obvious when your heart just isn't in it. If she had put her heart and soul into it and greeted everyone with a cheerful, "Good evening and a Merry Christmas," I bet her whole evening would have been different!

Put your heart and soul into what you do. It makes a world of difference.

14 November

Occupy your own space well! Yesterday someone said this to me, and it wasn't until I thought about it that I truly grasped what she meant. She told me, "Occupy your own space well, and everyone around you is happy." On reflection, do you think she meant know yourself, what you like and dislike, what makes you happy, where you are going, and what your focus is?

Help yourself first, so you can then help others. We are no good to anyone when we don't take care of ourselves. To occupy your space, I think, also means to fill your space to fullness. We are much more enjoyable to be around if people can see we are content and cheerful, and feel they have learnt something from us.

Occupy your space to fullness, and overflow onto others.

15 November

"Anxiety is the gap between the now and the later." Dr Wayne Dyer. This statement really struck me. How could I analyse it for me to understand it better? I likened it to crossing a road. You stand by the side of the road, waiting for a moment to cross. The side you are standing on is now, and the other side is the later. The anxiety is the road in the middle, with cars moving in both directions. Waiting can make you anxious and trying to pick the right time to cross can make you anxious. And when you've chosen to go, will you make it across before the next car comes along? The longer we spend in the gap, the more anxious we become. The sooner we arrive in the later, the better we will feel. Sounds very much like life! I think the key is to keep moving.

16 November

I recall my time swimming in the Red Sea in Egypt. When I jumped off the back of the boat with my snorkel, mask, and flippers, I was totally amazed by the cascade of colours not just in the fish but the plant life, coral, and water. I was in a world of my own, feeling comfortable, safe and secure, I spent hours swimming amongst the rainbow of another world.

Do you think we sometimes forget there is more to our world. If there is not a constant reminder, we tend to forget about the beauty of the unknown. It's not until you witness it that you can start to appreciate how beautiful our world is We need to make sure we witness more of our fascinating world and realise that we are a part of it.

17 November

I heard this statement from Dr Wayne Dyer the other day and loved it: "Success is advancing confidently in the direction of your own dreams, and endeavouring to live the life that you have imagined." Do we evaluate ourselves by what's around us? We live in a world that says you are what you have, what you do, and what you've accomplished and achieved.

Doing what you love and loving what you do is its own reward! That, for me, is advancing confidently in the direction of your own dreams. It's the process of doing it, living it, and loving it that appeals the most. That's what should *motivate* us, not the outcome of doing what we do. It's doing it that counts.

18 November

I was involved in a conversation recently where someone was explaining that even though she had a degree from university, she couldn't find a decent job. For me, that's like buying a car but not having the petrol to drive it around. The car is your qualifications, and the petrol is your drive, focus, determination, and your willingness and passion to move forward. You can have all the qualifications in the world, but they would never be enough if you don't have the ambition and drive to use them. The petrol is the most important part of this combination. You can build a car to get you from A to B, but the fuel, the energy, has to be in you from the beginning!

Do you have enough fuel within you to drive you where you want to go?

19 November

Have you ever felt so at peace with where your life is and who you are that you felt you could give up every material thing you have? This would have to be the ultimate test for feeling content. What would your life look like to be there, and how would you feel handing over your worldly possessions? It is worth having a think about it, because when you feel what it would be like to give it all away, you know whether you are in a good place or if there is still work to do.

Continue to stay true to yourself. Have a go, and see where you are with it. You may even surprise yourself.

20 November

A ten-year-old boy went to an ice-cream shop and asked the waiter how much a cone costs. The waiter told him fifty cents. The boy started counting how much he had in his purse and then he asked how much a small cup costs. The waiter said, "Forty cents." The boy asked for a small cup. He ate it, paid the bill, and left. When the waiter came to pick up the empty cup up, he was so touched, as the boy had left ten cents as a tip for him.

Try giving something to everyone out of whatever little you have.

21 November

Why are we intent on fixing things that don't need fixing? Or changing things that don't need changing? Why not stick to what works because it works. It's a bit like a recipe. This time of year, many traditional recipes are passed through the generations and still work and taste better than ever today, because they are the best. We still try to change the recipe, and it often doesn't taste quite the same.

When there is sometimes a need to change or fix something, then so be it. But we often change or fix for our benefit when it's not needed. A bit like reinventing the wheel. A proven recipe for success always has the same ingredients and has worked for thousands of years. So why change it?

Keep doing what has proven to work, and all will turn out great!

22 November

Why do we do it to ourselves? We beat ourselves up when things go wrong or as planned. We are too hard on ourselves when things happen to us that are out of our control. I once heard it's not the snakebite that kills you; it's the venom that enters your blood after the bite that kills. You can't be unbitten. Things happen, and the venom, your reaction to what happens, is what will or will not affect you!

23 November

This was written by my ten-year-old daughter, Liberty, for me to use for *Butterfly Whispers*. I was away on a trip and came home to this beautifully written piece. Bless her heart! She'd written it as if I had written it. How proud do you think I felt?

> A few days ago, when I was away in America, my daughter found a white feather. She was at my mum's house and looking around, when she saw the most lovely white feather. She told me when I came back that it reminded her of me, an angel. So I would just like to point out to you that if anyone you really love in your family is filled with happiness and peace, ask the person if he or she has ever experienced any happiness or peace in their life. If so, the individual has spread a lot of joy and love into the circle.

24 November

We are never given a wish without being given the power to make it happen! I love this quote. It makes me feel better about adversity to know I've only been given it, because I am strong enough to cope with it. So instead of thinking, *It's just one thing after another. Nothing's going right for me,* I think, *I wouldn't have been given this if I wasn't strong enough to cope.* So in fact, it's a compliment; the more adversity I face, the stronger I must be. This is a lot easier to cope with.

So if we are given the opportunity to wish for something, we must believe we have the power to turn that wish into a reality

25 November

If we all threw our problems in a pile and saw everyone else's, we'd grab ours back! Imagine everyone bagging up their problems and concerns and dumping them in a room. If you came back the next day, faced by different sized bags, I bet ours would be one of the smallest.

Grab your bag back before someone else does. Learn to deal with what you have been given, because it is our bag for a reason. Other people's problems are not going to build our characters or give value to our lives. We often feel our concerns are bigger than the next person's but that's not always the case. Own your bag, and learn to minimise your bag.

26 November

Please never worry about what anyone else says. Everyone is allowed his or her opinion. Only the opinions of those you love should matter to you. We often worry about what others may say to us or fear what others may think. As long as *we* are happy with what we think, how we look, how we behave, and how we speak, that is all that matters. The people who know us best and love us dearly can help us figure stuff out along the way. And because we love and respect them, their opinions count.

Be confident in your own self, and don't listen to what others say. You are perfection in your own right.

27 November

"Happiness is like a butterfly, when pursued, is always beyond our grasp, but, if you will sit down quietly, may alight upon you."

Nathaniel Hawthorne

In our busy lives we live today, what a difference it would make to sit down quietly and let happiness find you.

28 November

Take control. Our lives are vehicles, and we need to be in the driving seat and take control. Drive at a reasonable speed, but there will be times we need to drive faster or slower. If we keep at a steady pace, we are able to see what is going on around us. When we drive too fast, we are not able to enjoy life going on around us, and we get too tired.

Life is not a race, and we do not have to keep up with the person in front or stay ahead of the person behind. Let's enjoy the ride and share our journey with others.

29 November

After many years of searching, I am happy to be living my life on purpose. It is such a great feeling when we are clear about who we are, where we are going, and why we are here. Only when we know the answer to these three questions do we truly start living a life on purpose. When we have the answers to those questions, we are bolder in being free, free to be who we are, clear and free to know where we are going, and at peace in knowing why we are here. Answer these three questions for yourself, and you, too, can be living your life on purpose.

30 November

You gain strength, courage, and confidence through every experience in which you really stop to look fear in the face. You must do the thing you think you cannot do. With courage, you will dare to take risks, have the strength to be compassionate, and have the wisdom to be humble. Courage is the foundation of integrity. Courage is not the absence of fear but rather the judgement that something else is more important than fear.

Great joy comes from having the courage to do what frightens you.

Have the courage today to do what frightens you, however big or small, and feel like a winner.

1 December

Buddha once said, "If someone gives you a gift and you don't accept it, who does the gift belong to?" I often remind myself of this saying when someone says something I don't want to accept or does something to upset me. I imagine the person keeping it, so it is not mine, and it can't bother me. Equally, you become so much more aware of how you speak to people or behave towards them as they may be unaware of the Buddha principle and take onboard what you say or do as hurtful.

Keep this in mind as you travel through your day. And if people behave a certain way or say something hurtful, don't accept the gift, therefore, it doesn't belong to you.

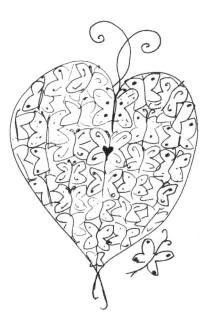

2 December

December is here; the madness begins. As if we are not busy enough with our daily lives, we now have lists as long as our arms of extra things to do. It can get all a bit overwhelming. A dear friend said to me earlier, and I love this analogy, "Think about when you overtake in a car. You change to a lower gear to go further and faster!"

The same should apply to us as people. To go further and faster, how do we change into a lower gear? As individuals, we need to find what suits us. It may be a bubble bath, meditation, playing a musical instrument, or going for a walk. Whatever your lower gear is, find it and use it to got you to go further and faster.

If you're like me, we sometimes keep going at such a pace that can only burn us out. It's so important to regroup and change to a lower gear, so we benefit greatly in the end. Change to a lower gear and go further and faster.

3 December

Words of wisdom from Mary Kay Ash:

> I'll always watch with great interest someone's first failure. It is the index of her life, the measure of her success power. The mere fact of her failure does not interest me very much, but how did she take defeat? Did she get up and go again with a determination that knows no defeat? A determined person cannot be kept from success. Place stumbling blocks in her way and she will take them for stepping stones and will climb to newer heights.

Mary Kay Ash was a very wise woman, a great visionary, and an excellent business woman. She empowered women to be the best they can be and to empower others to do the same. "Fail forward to success" was one of her favourite sayings.

May you always have what it takes to get up and go each time you fall.

4 December

Treat your body like a temple, not a bowling alley. If you had a very important guest come and live with you, what accommodations would you provide? Would you try and make your home look and feel as inviting as possible? Your spirit lives with you. Is your temple a suitable dwelling place for you? You don't have to be a model or an Olympic athlete; you just have to look after yourself. Exercise, get enough sleep, and eat well. For your mind, read books and watch the kind of films that encourage you to think properly. Now we have created the perfect place for us to stay.

You've created a temple worthy of you.

5 December

Isn't it amazing what can be done when you all pull together? Throughout the year, our village organises events to involve the whole community. There are May Day and summer fetes, but my favourite is Christmas. In the main high street, the shops stay open, and we all collect around the tree. Food and drinks are served. There is carol singing, and a temporary ice skating rink is set up in the village hall for the kids. Everyone gets wrapped up warmly.

It's great to spend the evening with friends and neighbours in the heart of the village. I feel it's really important for the children to get involved and see a community pull together. All the money raised goes back into the village, so everyone benefits. Teamwork makes the dream work, and so much more can be achieved when many people pull together.

6 December

He who walks with the wise grows wise, but a companion of fools suffers harm. Here are some simple guidelines to follow. Firstly, spend as much time as you can with people who encourage you. Secondly, as you befriend troubled people, be careful to do so on your own terms as much as possible. Thirdly, consistently ask yourself, "Am I drawing these people towards what I know is true, or are they drawing me away?" Keep in mind that it is easier to be pulled down than to be pulled up.

Like attracts like, so spend as much time as you can around the people you would like to be like.

7 December

Forgive yourself. A guilt trip is no vacation. Guilt is a heavy load to carry not only emotionally but also physically. It may be well-earned or just a lifelong accumulation of should haves. We can feel guilty about all sorts of things: not spending enough time with loved ones, maybe saying something that upset someone, or spending time relaxing. Whatever the source, guilt is an invisible stressor that won't lose its grip on you until you give up your hold on it.

Forgive yourself for what made you feel guilty. Or maybe you need to stop beating yourself up, as there is no need to feel guilty. Guilt is not a trip you want to take.

8 December

Break into song. Deep in the core of every human being is the joy of song. This seems to be intended to counterbalance the more routine and troublesome aspects of life, and it often relaxes you. Even if you can't carry a tune in a bucket, to burst into song can leave you feeling renewed and invigorated. In fact, singing is so energising that you can't help but tap your feet and spring into dance. It doesn't have to be any particular song. If you just start humming, a new song may bubble up from within.

I have been known to break into song and dance when my sister and I are in a shopping centre and a catchy song is playing. We look at each other and start singing and dancing. It really does make you feel good and often puts a smile on people's faces. Set your heart free and sing for joy!

9 December

Oprah Winfrey once said, "For every one of us that succeeds, it's only because someone showed them the way out." We can't all be famous, but each of us has it in us to be a light that shows the way. There may be times where we feel, or have felt, that who we are or what we know is not enough.

I believe that in our own way, we can be the lesson someone needs to learn to grow into who he or she was destined to be, or at least the next stage of the journey. We shine our light for others to follow. Who we are can be the example others need to see. When we think of all the people that shone their light for us to see, it's only fair we do the same for others.

10 December

I love giving gifts and could easily give each day. When we think about giving a gift, we think shopping. What about the most cherished gift? A smile, your time, or even a helping hand. These precious gifts cost nothing and are possibly the gifts that make the most difference to someone. These gifts come under the heading one size fits all, so we don't spend hours working out which one to get or getting a receipt in case the recipient wishes to return it. These gifts are priceless, and if the receiver of the gift doesn't want it, we don't lose out; it makes no difference to us. We are a better person for giving the gift in the first place.

Give your precious gifts away daily.

11 December

Acts of kindness can make a difference. As the story goes,

> During their second year of nursing school, their professor gave them a quiz. They breezed through the questions until they read the last one, "What is the first name of the woman who cleans the school?" Surely this was a joke. They had seen the cleaning woman several times, but how would they know her name? They handed in their papers, leaving the last question blank. Before the class ended, one student asked if the last question would count toward our grade. "Absolutely," the professor said. "In your careers you will meet many people. *All* are significant. They deserve your attention and care, even if all you do is say hello and smile." They've never forgotten that lesson. They also learned her name was Dorothy.

True acts of kindness really do make a difference.

12 December

Imagine your life as a mayonnaise jar. Fill it with golf balls. These represent what's important: your family, friends, and your health. When it's full with golf balls, put small pebbles in. These represent your job, your car, and your house, and they fit in around the golf balls. When you can't fit in more pebbles, fill your jar with sand. This represents minor things, like chores and errands. The sand is able to fit around the golf balls and pebbles.

Your jar is now full to the brim, but only because we put the golf balls in first, thon the pebbles, then the sand. Sometimes we till our lives with sand and with pebbles, leaving no room for the golf balls. When we put our family, friends, and our health first, there is always room for everything else.

Interestingly enough, when your jar is full to the top, pour in two cups of coffee. However busy and full our lives are, there is always room for a coffee with a friend.

13 December

A man was travelling home on a plane. The first warning of approaching problems came when the "fasten your seatbelts" sign flashed on. After a while, a calm voice said, "We shall not be serving drinks at this time, as we are expecting a little turbulence. Please make sure your seat belts are fastened." The man looked around the aircraft and saw many of the passengers were becoming apprehensive.

Later, the voice said, "We are so sorry that we are unable to serve meals at this time. The turbulence is still ahead of us." And then the storm broke. Within moments, the plane was being thrown around. It was lifted on terrific currents of air and then fell, as if about to crash. The man looked around and saw alarmed passengers and one little girl, very calmly reading her book.

After the storm blew over, the man asked the little girl why she wasn't frightened, She said, "'Cause my daddy's the pilot, and he's taking me home."

Have faith and know that whatever storms we may face, there is always a higher power looking out for you.

14 December

I love this time of year for the candles, among other things. Candles, to me, are a great symbol of how we should see ourselves. A candle needs both wax and wick to be able to burn. Too often we live our lives with either just wax or just wick and wonder. Then we wonder why it doesn't work.

Now we have both wax and wick, we need to light the wick with a flame, our desire. Only then are able to burn brighter and longer. We are also able to light others with our flame.

Burn brighter for longer today and all days.

15 December

Keep believing in yourself, and always remember I believe in you, too. Every goal that has ever been reached began with just one step and the belief it could be attained. Dreams really can come true, but they are most often the result of hard work, determination, and persistence. When the end of the journey seems impossible to reach, remember that all you need to do is take one more step. Stay focused on your goal, and remember each step will bring you a little closer. When the road becomes hard to travel and it feels as if you'll never reach the end, look deep inside your heart, and you will find strength you never knew you had. Believe in yourself, and I believe in you, too.

16 December

A farmer found an abandoned eagle's nest, and in it was an egg, still warm. He took the egg back to his farm and laid it in the nest of one of his hens. The egg hatched, and the baby eagle grew up with the other chickens. It pecked about the farmyard, scrambling for grain. It spent its life within the yard and rarely looked up. One day when it was very old, it lifted its head and saw above it an eagle soaring high above in the sky. Looking at it, the old creature sighed and said to itself, "If only I'd been an eagle."

Do you sometimes feel conditioned by your life around you? How do you know you're not an eagle? You'll only know if you try and soar. Chances are, you'll fly!

17 December

Heroes are not born; they are made. The ingredients are bravery, strength, and determination. I heard this yesterday in a children's film. What I love about this statement is that it says anyone can be a hero. I think many people think heroes are born or go through rigorous training. The truth of the matter is they are made, and they are everywhere. It is so important children realise this and believe they, too, can be heroes.

Nurture your bravery, strength, and determination. Who is your hero, and who are you a hero to?

18 December

Destiny is not the path given to us but the path we choose. Destiny can be perceived as a huge word, but it is really only what you choose it to be. Destiny is seven letters that can create your future. It's all how you see it.

Destiny is an exciting future, and one shaped to your liking. Every step you take forward is enough, and in time, know it's all a personalised journey. It is whatever you want it to be.

19 December

I was watching a Christmas movie with the children yesterday. One of the scenes was a mother taking her son to school. When she kissed him goodbye, she called to him, "Don't forget how special you are." This struck me as probably being the single most important thing a child should hear before they leave a parent. If you heard this every day at the beginning of your day, wouldn't it make such a difference?

Do we think of ourselves as special? If not, why not? We are all special to someone. Tell someone today, "Don't forget how special you are."

20 December

The happiest people are those who bring happiness to others. At this time of year, there are lots of occasions to be happy and spread Christmas cheer. So why can it be difficult to be cheerful and happy all year long? Do we need a reason to be happy? Why don't we use the reason that if we bring happiness to others, we'll all be happy? How lovely to be known as a happy, cheerful person. It needs to start somewhere, to get the ball rolling, so to speak. There is great satisfaction in contributing to someone else's happiness. We are helping ourselves to stay happy if we help others be happy.

21 December

As I sit looking out over a white garden, I can't help but think how beautiful and magical a snowfall makes everything look. However, how can something so beautiful also be so disruptive and dangerous? People struggle to get around, unable to get to work or complete final preparations for Christmas. It's too easy to get frustrated when there is nothing we can do about it. The kids just think it is the best thing, playing in the snow and building snowmen. When you do manage to get out in it, it is very easy to appreciate how magical where you live now looks.

Take time out in your day to appreciate your life around you. Whether you can do anything about it or not, it's a wonderful life!

22 December

Believe what you feel. Have you ever tried the trust experiment? You stand with your back to your partner. You are expected to fall back and rely on your partner to catch you. Most of us find this difficult and only let ourselves fall a few inches before stopping ourselves. If we close our eyes, cross our arms over our chest, and lean back, we can feel someone is there to catch us, more so than if our eyes are open. Closing our eyes makes the difference.

Sometimes, we cannot believe what we see. We have to believe what we feel. If we ever want others to trust us, we must feel we can trust them, too. Even when we're in the dark, even when we're falling.

23 December

While settling down after a busy day, I came across a programme, where two spoilt teenagers had been sent to live with two very strict parents and their children. The idea was for them to learn they can't go through life always getting their own way, to have respect for others, and to compromise. When these two teenagers arrived, their attitudes were so bad, I was cringing. Their manners were appalling, and they struggled to hold a conversation. At seventeen years old, I thought it was shocking.

The strict parents never gave in and taught them that to take, take, take was not the way forward. The teenagers didn't want to participate and stayed increasingly negative. What was amazing was the strict parents stayed consistent, made it clear what was acceptable, encouraged them, and made their stay fun. In one week, the teenagers got the message with the help from their own parents and wanted to be better people.

Whatever your conditioning, it is possible to turn things around.

24 December

Christmas angel. I heard this story and thought how amazing to be able to do this. A wealthy man researched his local area to find who needed help at this time of year. He bought groceries and gifts for underprivileged families, left them on the doorstep, knocked on the door, and hid. He paid hospital bills for people. He also arranged for a plumber to fix the heating in a couple's home, as she was nursing her husband in a home. This man would say, "Everyone needs to know that somebody cares."

His favourite time of year was Christmas. But there are so many people who dread this time of year. This man would say, "Who can I help?" and do all he could. How amazing this man is, a true Christmas angel.

25 December

On this day so many messages spring to mind, the gifts of giving, gratitude, love, and peace. But for some, it's none of these.

"God grant me the serenity to accept the things I cannot change. The courage to change the things I can and the wisdom to know the difference." Christmas can be so many things to so many people. Enjoy your Christmas.

26 December

Thankful is something that springs to mind today. Thankful for family, friends, and love. Thankful I am happy, healthy, and able to do whatever I choose. Nurture what you have, and be kind and caring to all around you. Fill every day with compassion, love, and understanding for others, and learn the lessons around us every day.

To be thankful is something that springs to mind today.

27 December

As our year draws to a close, I'm sure we are all remembering our year, good or bad. There are memories we'll cherish; some I'm sure we'll want to fade. It is a time to carry forward our triumphs and build on them in the following year. Learn from the days gone before, and these lessons will help us to grow for years to come.

Over a busy festive period and now a few days before the year ends, there is time to plan how you would like your year ahead to look personally, in business, or even simply to have a better year than the one before. Take time out to remember your highlights and what you would like to see happen for you in the year to come. Sort out where you are, so you can start a new year in some kind of order. Enjoy where you are right now; it is exactly where you are meant to be.

28 December

Do we give children the credit they deserve? Children are our future. Children often inspire me, because they are so raw, so open-minded. They believe anything is possible and have no limiting beliefs. The lessons we can learn from children are never-ending. Children see things as they are, because they are not conditioned. Adults sometimes see what we want to see and miss the real beauty. Children are born wanting to please; all they need is to be nurtured and loved. As adults, we can become too busy and stressed out with our daily lives, and we often know too much.

A child is learning all the time, as we are, but a child keeps an open mind. Children are our future. Let them inspire us!

29 December

Can you sense your Angel—the one that's by your side. The angel who is there, to comfort and to guide? If you allow yourself to trust, And to let yourself believe, you'll be showered with blessings, that you hardly will believe! For, the wings of an Angel are your shelter in a storm—A source of everlasting joy, as you awaken every morn.

So, become aware today of this gift sent from above—The Angel at your side who's the embodiment of love.

Anon

May you always have an angel by your side.

30 December

"Life is like riding a bicycle," was advice Einstein gave his son. "To keep your balance you must keep moving." If it's good enough for Einstein, it's good enough for me. How sensible is this. Of course, we need to keep moving to keep our balance on our bicycle.

How many times do we feel we have fallen off our bicycle? Maybe it was during some painful and trying circumstances. Maybe someone or something has knocked us off our bicycle. We get straight back on and keep moving! By moving, we also build momentum which will keep us going through trickier times. The wheels on our bicycle need little effort to get going. Start pedalling, and keep on keeping on.

31 December

"If you tend to see yourself as a nobody, you are going to find that others will take you at your own self-evaluation. That's why I constantly tell you that when somebody asks, "How are you?" I want you to say, "Great!" No matter what. If you don't think you are great, nobody else will either."

Mary Kay Ash

Thank you for taking the time to read my book. You are GREAT!

Lightning Source UK Ltd.
Milton Keynes UK
UKOW06f1302101213

222713UK00003BA/22/P